EDWARD
& SOPHIE
A Royal Wedding

EDWARD & SOPHIE

❧ *A Royal Wedding* ❧

JUDY PARKINSON

CB

CONTEMPORARY BOOKS

Library of Congress Cataloging-in-Publication Data

Parkinson, Judy.
 Edward & Sophie: a royal wedding / Judy Parkinson.
  p. cm.
 ISBN 0-8092-2428-3
  1. Edward, Prince, son of Elizabeth II, Queen of Great Britain. 2. Marriages of royalty
and nobility—Great Britain—History—20th century. 3. Weddings—Great Britain—
History—20th Century. 4. Princes—Great Britain—Biography. 5. Rhys-Jones, Sophie,
1965– I. Title. II. Title: Edward and Sophie.
DA591.A45E395 1999
941.085'092—dc21   99-31500
[B]   CIP

Designed and typeset by Martin Bristow

First published in Great Britain in 1999 by Michael O'Mara Books Limited

First published in the United States in 1999 by Contemporary Books
A division of NTC/Contemporary Publishing Group, Inc.
4255 West Touhy Avenue, Lincolnwood (Chicago), Illinois 60646-1975 U.S.A.

Copyright © 1999 by Michael O'Mara Books Limited

Printed and bound in Germany

International Standard Book Number: 0-8092-2428-3

99 00 01 02 03   17 16 15 14 13 12 11 10 9 8 7 6 5 4 3 2 1

HALF-TITLE PAGE: *Although Prince Edward actually asked Sophie Rhys-Jones*
to marry him in December 1998, the formal announcement — and invitation
to the paparazzi for the inevitable photo call — did not go out until
the first week of 1999.

FRONTISPIECE: *Wednesday, 6 January 1999 – HRH The Prince Edward*
and his fiancée, Sophie Rhys-Jones, pose for photographers at St James's Palace
on the official announcement of their engagement.

FACING PAGE: *The formal announcement of the couple's engagement,*
issued by Buckingham Palace on 6 January 1999.

⤳ Contents ⤴

THE ENGAGEMENT

6

THE BRIDEGROOM

16

THE BRIDE

52

ROYAL WEDDINGS

86

THE WEDDING

108

Acknowledgements

128

BUCKINGHAM PALACE

THE FOLLOWING ANNOUNCEMENT IS ISSUED BY THE PRESS SECRETARY TO THE QUEEN

The Queen and The Duke of Edinburgh are delighted to announce the engagement of their youngest son, Prince Edward, to Miss Sophie Rhys-Jones.

The couple sought the permission of their respective parents between Christmas and the New Year. Both families are thrilled at the news.

No decision has been taken yet regarding the venue and date for the wedding. However, Prince Edward and Miss Rhys-Jones hope that it might be possible to use St. George's Chapel, Windsor, in the late Spring or Summer.

To be released at 1000 hours GMT, Wednesday 6th January, 1999

Royal Web site: www.royal.gov.uk

❧ The Engagement ❧

ROYAL WEDDINGS are not like other weddings. There is nothing even remotely ordinary about them, for above all they are majestic public occasions loaded with historical significance. On the afternoon of Saturday, 19 June 1999, the world watched as His Royal Highness the Prince Edward led his bride down the aisle of St George's Chapel, Windsor. Now, after the pageantry of that – admittedly private – ceremony, the House of Windsor enters a new era in its history. This triumphantly happy couple are perfect symbols of modern royalty for the twenty-first century.

People all over the world continue to be fascinated by the fortunes of Britain's most famous family, and not least because popular interest in the life of the Queen's children will not fade away. This marriage is not about the succession to the throne, as had been the case when the world watched the wedding of the Prince and Princess of Wales in 1981. That responsibility now rests with Prince Charles and the succeeding generation in the person of Prince William. Prince Edward is now removed from direct line of succession to the throne, which means that he and his new wife can concentrate on their own priorities, of which the first is to build a loving, modern, and working partnership. Their marriage is, however, extremely significant because it will embody a new agenda for the Windsors in the years ahead, after one of the most turbulent decades of the Queen's reign.

The foundations of the monarchy were seismically shifted by the divorces of Edward's sister, Princess Anne, and his brothers Prince Charles and Prince

Andrew. There was unprecedented global interest in the activities and ultimate fall from grace of both the Queen's daughters-in-law, compounded, in
the case of the Princess of Wales, by her tragic death in August 1997. As the
Queen herself has publicly admitted, these events have been a source of great
sadness, worry and disappointment to her; furthermore, she is only too well
aware that they have provoked a widespread and passionate debate about the
role of the monarchy in a modern democratic society. The royal family faces
the challenge not only of sustaining its existence into the next century, but
also of creating a new meaning for itself. Prince Edward's marriage will,
inevitably, be a part of that process. The pressures on the couple to make a
success of their union are immense – if it is important for their future happiness, it is vital for the royal family.

Family life has been central to the British monarchy for well over a century, a source of its strength and an indicator of its wellbeing. Since Queen
Victoria's day the public have looked to them to uphold family values.
As Prince Philip explained, 'If you are going to have a monarchy, you have got
to have a family, and the family has got to be in the public eye.' Attitudes have
changed, however, generally rather faster than the monarchy has been able to
adapt. The British public no longer respects appearances as once they used to.
They do not regard royals or politicians as their betters. They will not tolerate

Prince Edward and his brother, Prince Andrew,
in suitably festive mood before the royal
family's traditional Christmas Day service
at Sandringham Parish Church in 1993.
By then, news of Edward's relationship with
Sophie Rhys-Jones had reached the media,
three months after he had first met her.

RIGHT: *The royal family quickly warmed to Sophie, and it is greatly to her credit that she has skilfully mastered all sorts of arcane points of royal etiquette. She was invited to stay at Windsor Castle not long after first meeting Prince Edward, and since then she has stayed at Balmoral, Sandringham and, as here, on board HMY* Britannia, *before the Royal Yacht was taken out of the Queen's service and decommissioned from the Royal Navy in late 1997.*

BELOW: *Being Seen Together In Public – even if Sophie has still dutifully positioned herself the equivalent of the traditional two paces behind . . . Edward and his girlfriend watch a pantomime-horse race during the Duke of Edinburgh's Award Charity Race Day at Ascot in July 1995.*

double standards in public life. They require their leaders to represent them, rather than simply advocate a particular lifestyle. As recent events have shown, the royal family is now more answerable to the public than ever before, and its members must modify their ways if they are to retain a meaningful position in British life.

At over five years, the courtship of Edward and Sophie is by far the longest wooing by any member of the royal family. From the beginning, the hallmark of the relationship has been discretion; indeed, it has been conducted with an almost compulsive desire for privacy. Although the press had known about

and reported the relationship for years, the announcement of the couple's engagement in January 1999 was Prince Edward's first public articulation of his firm commitment to Sophie. 'We are the best of friends,' he said without the least hesitation, 'and we happen to love each other very much.' It was yet another indication that the couple know their own minds, and that, together, they are definitely in control of their destiny.

Like all good love stories, the romance began with a chance meeting. In September 1993, when the tennis star Sue Barker had to pull out of a charity real-tennis event at the Queen's Club in West London, PR assistant Sophie Rhys-Jones stepped in for the photo call with Prince Edward. By the time he left the club that fateful afternoon, the Prince had made certain that he had Sophie's phone number. A flurry of discreet dates followed, and for some weeks their friendship was cloaked in secrecy. In that time they became inseparable, and Sophie received the ultimate mark of approval when she was invited to join the royal family for church services, taking her place in their private pews in St George's Chapel, Windsor Castle, years later to be the scene of her midsummer marriage.

When details of the relationship emerged three months after their first meeting, Edward did his utmost to protect not only himself, but also Sophie, from press intrusion. A few days before Christmas 1993 he sent an open letter to editors appealing that they spare them the harassment that he believed had harmed other royal romances; he added that he and Sophie were 'good friends' but that they had no plans to marry. With the press in full cry, however, he realized that in future they would both have to be cautious, and informal suppers at Sophie's West Kensington flat had to stop. If she ever felt insecure as a result of the need for discretion or the extravagant length of Edward's courtship, however, she wisely kept her counsel. As time passed Sophie began to appear with Edward in public, making her first appearance on a royal occasion at the wedding of the Queen's niece, Lady Sarah Armstrong-Jones, to Daniel Chatto in the summer of 1994. Weddings display the royal family at its most tribal and, as she had become used to doing, Sophie walked

ABOVE LEFT: *That first photo . . . Like all good love stories, the romance began with a chance meeting. On 13 September 1993, when the tennis star Sue Barker had to pull out of a charity real-tennis event at the Queen's Club in West London, PR girl Sophie Rhys-Jones stepped into the breach, posing with Prince Edward for the press shots. This would be the most relaxed and intimate picture of the couple together until the announcement of their engagement over five years later.*

ABOVE LEFT AND ABOVE: *Whatever the media had said over the previous five years about the couple's relationship, there could be no doubting their happiness on the day the engagement was announced. 'It's impossible to understand why it has taken me this long . . .' remarked the Prince.*

RIGHT: *Thursday, 7 January 1999 – Sophie, besieged by journalists and photographers, receives a police escort as she arrives at the Mayfair offices of R-JH, the public-relations company she co-founded in 1997, the day after the announcement. The flowers are from one of her legion of well-wishers, but for Sophie it is very much business as usual.*

two steps behind Edward, who gave no outward sign of his affection for her. This is the way of the Windsors, and it is greatly to Sophie's credit that she has skilfully mastered all sorts of arcane points of royal etiquette.

Sophie put her organizational skills to good effect when she arranged a surprise thirtieth-birthday party for Edward at the Savoy Hotel in March 1994. It is a mark of their excellent relationship that the Queen, who appreciates Sophie's candid and pleasant manner and her businesslike approach to life, accepted the young woman's invitation to attend as a surprise guest. By now Sophie had rooms at Buckingham Palace – something that would not have been possible without the Queen's approval – and she and Edward were appearing together in public with increasing frequency. Yet despite the approval of Her Majesty and the couple's obvious closeness, there were no signs of an engagement.

As the months passed, Sophie dedicated herself to setting up her own public-relations firm while Edward concentrated on establishing his television production company. Their charity work is also an extremely important feature of the couple's lives, and particularly their involvement with the

Macmillan Nurses and the Duke of Edinburgh's Award Scheme. It is clear that both have been laying firm foundations for the life that lies ahead of them as part of a modern working monarchy. At the time, however, they maintained a polite silence about their future plans together.

Because of the nature of his personality, and in the light of the experiences of his sister and both his brothers, Edward was determined to do things his way, and resisted the sort of pressure that was placed on Prince Charles. Thus what many regarded as procrastination was in fact simple resoluteness, a determination to wait until he and Sophie felt that the time was exactly right for both of them. There were other factors, too, not the least of which was that, in the aftermath of the tragic death of the Princess of Wales, it would have been inappropriate, at best, to make any wedding announcement until after a decent interval of time had elapsed.

The Prince planned his surprise proposal down to the last detail. When he swept Sophie off to the Bahamas just before Christmas 1998, she had no idea that by the end of the week she would be a royal bride-in-waiting. In exotic isolation on Windermere Island, a favourite location for many royal holidays, Edward and Sophie spent many happy hours swimming, walking and relaxing. Then, on the last night of the vacation, Edward, on bended knee, asked Sophie to marry him, and received in return her much quoted reply, 'Yes, yes please.' Gallantly, he showed his respect for tradition by insisting that he should ask Sophie's father for his permission to marry her before they made their joy known to the world.

Edward and Sophie's appearance before the media following the announcement of their engagement on 6 January 1999 was a most polished performance. They maintained a pleasant and polite, almost friendly, attitude towards their press interrogators, and thereby showed a poise and confidence all too often missing from previous photo calls proclaiming a royal

ABOVE LEFT: *More flowers for the royal bride-to-be as she reaches her office shortly after nine o'clock on the morning of her thirty-fourth birthday, 20 January 1999.*

ABOVE: *Prince Edward's dislike of media attention has at times amounted almost to a phobia. None the less, the constant attentions of journalists and photographers are a feature of life for modern royalty, as is clear from this shot of the Prince at the Boat Show in London, after the announcement of his engagement — an announcement guaranteed to increase the press's interest in him.*

FACING PAGE: *An exclusive photograph, never published before, of a relaxed and confident Sophie Rhys-Jones. With great style her wardrobe reflects her busy working life, as well as the need for her to dress for formal royal occasions.*

engagement. Beyond their charm and their obvious affection for one another, however, it has not gone unnoticed that the couple have not only carefully avoided rumour and speculation about their relationship, but have also refused to let anyone force them into a decision they did not wish to make, or before they were ready to make it. As Edward said, 'It's impossible to understand why it has taken me this long, but I don't think it would have been right before, and I don't think she would have said yes.'

Prince Edward is the youngest of the Queen's children, and the last of them to wed. This union, however, unlike those of his sister and brothers, is capable of existing – indeed, to a considerable extent, will exist – completely outside Court circles. Here is no dynastic marriage of convenience, no dangerous liaison with cousins or courtiers. Lacking an aristocratic family tree or any royal connections, the far from blue-blooded Sophie brings with her a refreshing awareness of the world and an experience of everyday life which, however hard they try, the Queen's children can never quite know. Above all, and although the world inside and outside the Court has changed beyond recognition, the signs are set fair. This new royal partnership is a blend of friendship and business, as well as love. At the dawn of the new millennium, it marks the optimistic beginning to a new era for the British monarchy.

FACING PAGE: *Sophie undoubtedly has an eye for classic style, elegantly matching modern suits with fine jewellery and spangled details. She is neither an aristocrat nor a fashion plate, however, but very much her own woman with her own definite, if understated, style. She chose one of her favourite designers, Tomasz Starzewski, to tailor this elegant outfit for the engagement announcement.*

BELOW: *The pressures upon the couple to make a success of their marriage are immense. Furthermore, that success is important not just for their future happiness together, but because the marriage embodies a new agenda for the House of Windsor in the years ahead, as the royal family comes to terms with its changing role.*

~ The Bridegroom ~

FACING PAGE: *Prince Edward at the beginning of his marathon real-tennis game during the charity event at the Queen's Club at which he first met Sophie. Real tennis, the ancient form of the game, is played on an indoor court equipped with various 'hazards'; it is a favourite of the Prince's, who has done much to raise its profile.*

PRINCE EDWARD is a child of the sixties, a decade that saw a sea change not just in the way royal events were reported, but in the attitudes of the media – and thus ultimately of the public – towards the royal family itself. From the day he was born he has been close to the centre of a media revolution that has fostered fundamental changes in the British monarchy. His is the story of a young man with a dream to be an ordinary bloke, but who happened to be born a prince, and his complex personality illustrates this contradiction in his constant struggle for individuality. He has always wanted to live a normal life with the freedom to do the everyday things that most people take for granted, yet he has always had a sense of his own royalty, a kind of inner commitment. He personifies a delicate balance between duty and personal ambition, public and private life.

In return, the Prince's motives have been scrutinized throughout his life, and even his manhood or his sexuality have been questioned, such speculation

PREVIOUS PAGE, LEFT AND FACING PAGE: *A series of photographs of the royal family taken in the gardens at Windsor on the Queen's thirty-ninth birthday, 21 April 1965. Prince Edward, then just over a year old, is seen (previous page) peering out of his pram, steadied by the Duke of Edinburgh and his fourteen-year-old sister, Princess Anne, while the Queen and the five-year-old Prince Andrew look at flowers; (left) Prince Andrew offers his younger brother a daffodil, to the amusement of the sixteen-year-old Prince Charles; (facing page) the entire family poses in the early spring sunshine. This was the sort of image of the royal family that persisted until the late sixties, when the Queen's permitting of a television documentary about their life and work irrevocably altered public and media attitudes towards the monarchy.*

being one of the most marked effects of that media revolution. As a result, he displays an almost obsessive need for privacy, and has on occasions made it clear that he is prepared to defend it. The reasons for this are not hard to find. The seeds of his dislike, even resentment, of intrusion into his private life were sown when he was a small boy. Having been a child star of the TV documentary *Royal Family*, avidly watched by millions of viewers when it was screened in 1969, he has led his whole life in the media spotlight.

Prince Edward was born on Tuesday, 10 March 1964 in the Belgian Suite at Buckingham Palace, the fourth and youngest child of the Queen and the Duke of Edinburgh. It was a remarkable occasion since, for the first time in modern history, a royal father was present at the birth of his child. Attitudes were changing in the mid-sixties, and the Queen was determined to share at least something of the experience of childbirth with Prince Philip. Yet only a few years earlier it would have been unthinkable, distasteful even, to have allowed anyone apart from the entourage of doctors and midwives to attend the birth.

In due course the baby was christened Edward Anthony Richard Louis, some four years after his older brother Prince Andrew and fifteen and sixteen

years, respectively, after Princess Anne and Prince Charles. At the beginning of her reign the Queen had become somewhat distant from Charles and Anne, often putting duty before family; indeed, they hardly recognized her when she returned after a marathon six-month tour that she and Prince Philip undertook in the early fifties. Besides this, she had been a rather aloof and distant mother to her two older children, something that reflected the way in which she herself had been brought up. With the younger boys, however, things were rather different, and she was to attend almost every important event in their early lives. By the beginning of the sixties she had become altogether more confident in her role as monarch, and not least because it was some years since she had succeeded, at the tender age of twenty-five, to the throne. The later arrival, after a considerable gap, of Andrew and Edward, her second family as she called them, gave her a new chance to exercise her maternal

instincts. Thus the younger boys were not confined for most of the time to the nursery with Nanny, and they enjoyed a great deal more motherly pampering than had their older siblings.

The curtain was about to rise upon a dramatic new episode in the royal saga, however. It all started with a man in a white coat in a laboratory. In 1968 an unscrupulous technician at the photo laboratories to which the royal family sent their own snaps for processing, made a second copy of the prints of Edward as a baby and sold them to *Paris Match*. At once photographs of the family group taken by Prince Philip and Princess Anne were splashed all over magazines in Europe and America, while the *Daily Express* featured a picture of Edward in his mother's arms on the front cover. The genie had been let out of the royal bottle, never to be forced back in again. With equal measures of sententiousness and self-justification, the editorial in the offending issue of the *Express* proclaimed: 'They are probably the most delightful pictures of the Royal Family ever taken. The *Daily Express* publishes them confident that it is only fitting that the British people should share a picture series that will catch the interest of the world.'

The *Express* was right. The world was entranced – and the royal family was appalled, although the Queen did not go to law over this invasion of privacy as she almost certainly would today; in 1968 it was deemed undignified for the royal family to answer back. Publication of the family pictures, and especially those showing the infant Edward in the informal setting of the Queen's boudoir, marked a significant change in public attitudes towards the royal family, and effectively set the tone of royal reporting for the next thirty

years and more. The public, it seemed, wanted to know everything about their sovereign and her family, and the media were only too happy to oblige.

The royal family are traditionally slow to change their habits, and most of them resisted pressure to do so. The notable exception was Prince Philip, who appreciated that the public were interested in the whole family – an interest that he believes is central to the monarchy – and who therefore encouraged a little more accessibility so that people could identify with each generation in his family, rather than just with the Sovereign and a handful of other senior members. Yet both the Queen and Prince Philip himself were unsure as to how to react when this openness was put into practice, largely because they were used to stage-managing royal appearances as and when they chose, not to performing for a public who seemed to want to direct the show themselves. Their natural inclination, therefore, was to maintain their genteel style, and to continue their duties in the understated manner, and with all the formality, of their parents' generation. Thus vulgar public displays continued to be frowned upon – to such an extent that photographs of the young Prince Andrew had been restricted, thereby provoking rumours in the Continental press that there was something to hide. The public, meanwhile, were clamouring for more. It was clear that the royal family were going to have to confront the uncomfortable issue of more public exposure.

The Palace public-relations solution was to invite the BBC's television cameras in to look at the Queen's life and work. While this was a landmark in royal history, it also proved to be the first instalment in an everyday tale of royal folk that was to run and run. According to the Queen's Press Secretary

FACING PAGE, ABOVE: *Princess Margaret with her daughter, Lady Sarah Armstrong-Jones, her nephew, Prince Edward, her son David, Viscount Linley, and Princess Anne, looks out for the photographers as their train leaves Liverpool Street for the journey to Sandringham in late December 1966.*

FACING PAGE, BELOW: *Three years later, and a very assured Prince Edward, two months short of his sixth birthday, shakes hands with an official as he arrives at Liverpool Street from Sandringham, January 1970.*

ABOVE: *Prince Edward arrives at King's Cross from Balmoral in November 1970.*

RIGHT: *Less formally, the seven-year-old Prince hugs a black labrador pup during a visit to the Balmoral kennels. To mark his eighteenth birthday in 1982, he was featured on the cover of* Dog World *with his black labrador, Francis; 'The dog got more mail than I did,' he remarked later.*

LEFT: *Despite the fourteen-year gap in their ages, Edward is closest to his sister Anne. This photograph of her on the balcony of Buckingham Palace was taken on the day of her marriage to Captain Mark Phillips in November 1973. Her page, Prince Edward, was then nine, just two months older than the bridesmaid, his cousin Lady Sarah Armstrong-Jones.*

BELOW: *Prince Edward on the same balcony just a few months earlier, with Prince Andrew and the Duke of Kent behind him, stands beside the Queen and the Duke of Edinburgh after the ceremony of Trooping the Colour, June 1973.*

at the time, William Heseltine, the 105-minute documentary 'enlarged and subtly changed the public's idea of what the Queen and her family are really like.' The programme was also interpreted as the most fantastic piece of eavesdropping of all time. As for the young Prince Edward, having a film crew around for eight months had a profound effect upon him, and was to shape his future career; moreover, he has nurtured an equivocal relationship with the media ever since. Some 28 million viewers of the final programme, *Royal Family*, saw Edward throwing snowballs, going on picnics, playing with puppies, decorating the Christmas tree and buying sweets in the village with his own pocket money. As a cherubic five-year-old, the youngest of the Queen's children stole the show.

The BBC documentary marked the end of an age of media innocence for the royal family, an innocence never to be recaptured. Until then, royal children had been able to go out and about relatively unrecognized. Thus Edward and his cousins might go on excursions to the museums, and be ignored by a public blissfully unaware of their identities. The year of his birth had been a particularly good one for royal cousins. Along with Edward, Lady Sarah

At another such ceremony, the Queen, again in the uniform of Colonel-in-Chief of all five regiments of Foot Guards, explains a detail to her youngest son. At the beginning of her reign, the Queen had been somewhat distant and aloof from her two older children. The later arrival of Princes Andrew and Edward, by which time she was more confident in her role as monarch, gave her a new chance to exercise her maternal instincts, and she was to attend almost every important event in their early lives.

Armstrong-Jones, Lady Helen Windsor and James Ogilvy were all born in 1964, which meant that Edward enjoyed an active social life from the start. Later James would accompany Edward to his pre-prep school, and Sarah became his closest childhood friend. They would all spend Christmas together at Windsor Castle, where they had great fun riding bicycles up and down the green corridor lined with priceless antiques. Sarah's older brother and the ringleader in their games, David, Viscount Linley, actually broke one of the priceless Ming vases.

If he got on well with his cousins, Edward often had to compete for attention with his rowdier brother, Andrew. Although close in age, the temperaments of the two brothers were wildly contrasting. Andrew was a boisterous and mischievous prankster, while Edward's innocent cherubic looks precluded his gaining such a reputation, even if his behaviour had merited it. There has never been any animosity between them, but they were not close. Prince Charles has been a remote brother, both in age and attitude, although he wrote his charming children's story, *The Old Man of Lochnagar*, for his younger brothers. Edward is closest to his sister Anne, and shares her love of riding. Despite the difference in their ages, she used to write him long chatty letters when he was at boarding school, and usually addressed him by some affectionate nickname.

Edward's education began at Gibbs's pre-preparatory school in Kensington, which he had the great advantage of attending with his cousin and best friend, James Ogilvy. Next was Heatherdown Preparatory School, near Windsor, to which Prince Andrew also went. It was here that Edward first took to the boards – as Mole in *Toad of Toad Hall* – when he was eleven. He was spirited and confident, very different from the shy boy who had arrived at the school three years before in 1972. At school he showed himself to be very independent, and from the start made it clear that he expected no special

ABOVE LEFT: *Watching the cross-country event at the Badminton Horse Trials in April 1973. From left to right: the Duke of Beaufort, Prince Edward (then nine), Lord Linley (almost obscured by the Queen's shoulder), Prince Andrew, the Queen and the Duke of Edinburgh. Edward shares his sister's and his mother's love for riding and their interest in horses.*

ABOVE: *At Badminton with his mother again, this time watching the veterinary inspection before the show-jumping in April 1978.*

ABOVE RIGHT: *The Queen and her youngest son at the Royal Windsor Horse Show in May 1995. By then the Prince's relationship with Sophie Rhys-Jones was nearly two years old.*

RIGHT: *A formal group portrait of the royal family, taken at Buckingham Palace in November 1972. The Duke of Edinburgh, appreciating that the public were interested in the family as a whole, felt that a certain amount of openness could only benefit the monarchy. Nevertheless, Prince Edward is the only member of the family in this photograph who appears to be not the least bit apprehensive.*

privileges. He made friends easily and, besides acting and other interests, was also a good rugby player. Generally Edward enjoyed his school days, something probably made easier by the fact that he was largely spared the intrusion of journalists and photographers, unlike Prince Charles, whose schooldays were dogged by reporters, and his every sip of cherry brandy analysed and recorded for posterity.

The prep schools were the Queens' choice for her two younger sons, but it was their father who decided that the boys should attend Gordonstoun, his own alma mater, set on the windswept coast of the Moray Firth. The Duke believed that all his sons would benefit from the school's accent on individual development and community service, particularly because he considered that public schools like Eton encouraged in their pupils an elitist philosophy that in turn led them to an unearned and unwarranted sense of privilege. Edward passed his Common Entrance exams and started at Gordonstoun at the age of thirteen. He learnt how to get on with people from different backgrounds and it was here that his nascent love of the theatre blossomed. The only similarity Edward's path through school had with that of his brother, Prince Charles, was that he too became Guardian, as the head boy at Gordonstoun is known. Charles had detested the place, where he was miserable, lonely and bullied. When Edward joined the school, however, ten years after his eldest brother had left, it was a very different scene, and not least because by then it accepted girls, which, among other things, made putting on plays much easier. Even so, some of the Spartan rituals of Charles's day were maintained,

Her Majesty Queen Elizabeth the Queen Mother, flanked by Prince Edward and Prince Andrew, arrives at St Paul's Cathedral for a Service of Thanksgiving to mark the Silver Jubilee of the Queen's accession to the throne, 7 June 1977.

RIGHT: *Prince Andrew (left) and the thirteen-year-old Prince Edward talk to officers and men of the Royal Marines at Plymouth Hoe in August 1977 – an unhappy augury for the younger prince's future, as matters would turn out.*

BELOW: *On the day of her seventy-ninth birthday, the Queen Mother is joined outside her London residence, Clarence House, by three of her grandchildren, Prince Edward, Lady Sarah Armstrong-Jones, and Lord Linley. Since 1970, when the Queen and the Duke of Edinburgh left their car and walked among the crowds in Wellington during a tour of New Zealand, 'walkabouts' have become an increasingly important – and expected – part of royal life. The outings of the Queen Mother on her birthdays, during which she talks to members of the crowd and receives flowers and gifts from them, are among the most popular of all.*

so that Edward still had to suffer the eighty-yard dawn run followed by a cold shower.

At Gordonstoun, Edward characteristically kept his emotions under control, and was inclined to take himself quite seriously, sometimes in a very regal manner. His housemaster, James Thomas, remembered, 'People who did not know him would have probably seen him as a bit strait-laced, which he was not – he had a jolly good sense of humour. But he could come across as perhaps taking his responsibilities too seriously.' The young prince had a tendency to be pompous – a quality that still surfaces at times – but he was a very gregarious youngster who got on with pretty well everyone. He had to. There was no privacy, and he and his fellows slept in a cramped dormitory, head to toe with twenty-five other boys, in a room no bigger than the nursery at Buckingham Palace.

Academically Edward outshone the rest of the family. He passed nine O levels and three A levels – in history, English and politics with economics – as well as an S level in history, leading the tabloids to dub him 'Educated Eddie'. He was, too, fearless on the rugby pitch, although his first passion remained drama. He became a leading light in the drama department and was in the vanguard of many experimental productions at school, producing and acting

A formal group of the Queen and her family taken in September 1979, when Prince Edward was fifteen and in his second year at his public school, Gordonstoun. In the foreground is a royal 'dorgi', a dachshund-corgi cross.

in smaller, more demanding plays than the usual large-scale school extrava-ganzas. He was in good company. His contemporaries included Jason Connery, son of Sean Connery, who directed him in one of the productions and who recalled of his royal contemporary, 'He never minds being told what to do. He listens hard so he can learn fast.'

Edward's overcrowded schedule also included an Air Cadet Proficiency gliding course at RAF Benson, Oxfordshire, in 1980, taking his private pilot's licence two years later, shortly after his eighteenth birthday, and he was head of Gordonstoun's ATC (Air Training Corps) in his final year. Although his A-level results suffered in consequence, he gained a place at Jesus College, Cambridge, to study archaeology and anthropology, although he changed to history in his second year.

Away from school, Edward had an endless number of options for holiday activities. He enjoyed sailing at Cowes and cruising on the Royal Yacht *Britannia* around the Western Isles of Scotland, riding at Windsor, shooting at Balmoral and Sandringham, fishing at Balmoral, swimming in the pools at Windsor and Buckingham Palace, and riding and haymaking at Gatcombe Park, the Gloucestershire estate of his sister and her then husband, Captain Mark Phillips. He frequently went skiing in Austria as a guest of his former

After the ceremony of Trooping the Colour in June 1985, Prince Edward stands with other members of the royal family on the balcony of Buckingham Palace to watch the flypast. Prince Charles, standing between his sister and his wife, holds his younger son, Prince Harry, then not quite a year old; Prince William, four days short of his third birthday, stands in front of his father.

headmaster at Heatherdown and his family. He learnt to sail and water ski, and to drive four-wheel-drive vehicles at Sandringham. While in London Lady Sarah Spencer, Prince Charles's latest flame (and elder sister of the woman he would later marry, Lady Diana Spencer), used to take him to the cinema to see James Bond films, and he enjoyed unfettered shopping trips in Chelsea and Kensington with his great friend and cousin, Lady Sarah Armstrong-Jones. When not engaged in this hectic round of activities he loved reading and was an avid radio fan, carrying his Roberts set around with him in a special wooden case. He enjoyed listening to middle-of-the-road pop music, especially Abba, whose music would feature heavily in the discos he organized for his cousins at Windsor Castle – much to their amusement. The whole family, however, cousins included, loved watching the one-man shows that he wrote and performed himself.

Having always had a special affinity with his sister, Princess Anne, Edward spent many holidays with her at Gatcombe Park, where he had his own pony, an Arab mare given to the Queen on one of her tours of the Middle East. Although not as expert a rider as the Princess, who represented Britain at the Olympic Games, he was a good horseman none the less, and they rode together every day. While this closeness between brother and sister might be expected, perhaps rather more surprising is the fact that Prince Edward has always enjoyed a close rapport with his father. Prince Philip was not as stern as he appeared, nor was Edward as delicate as his youthful looks suggested. The Duke taught his youngest son to shoot, with the result that he became an extremely enthusiastic field sportsman. Unhampered by the trappings of royalty, father and son would spend hours crawling among the reeds and marshes on wildfowling expeditions.

If these were private moments, public exposure was never far away. To mark his eighteenth birthday in 1982, Edward was given the dubious honour of being featured on the cover of the magazine *Dog World* with his labrador,

ABOVE LEFT: *Prince Edward left Gordonstoun in 1982, and in September that year went to New Zealand to teach as part of his pre-university year. In his post-school and Cambridge days he was never to be short of enjoyable things to do. Here, looking very much the young man about town, he watches a flypast during a charity event at Ascot.*

ABOVE: *The Prince has always enjoyed sailing, and is seen here relaxing on board the British yacht* Aquavit *during the annual regatta at Cowes. Cowes Week had other advantages besides sailing, however, for it was the scene of two romantic encounters for the first time – with Romy Adlington in 1983, and Georgia May in 1986.*

Francis. 'The dog got more mail than I did,' he said. He need not have worried about lack of fan mail, however. Shortly afterwards an American magazine ran a feature on teenage princes of Europe, which included a photograph and biography of Edward along with those of the likes of Prince Albert of Monaco and Prince Filipe of Spain. Readers were invited to write to him at Buckingham Palace. Thousands of letters had to be carted off in tea chests.

With Gordonstoun behind him and a place at Cambridge assured, a royal gap year now beckoned. As Prince Edward himself recalls, 'There was a pattern and New Zealand was a part of it. I knew I was going to university, I knew I had secured my place with the Royal Marines, I knew what I was going to be doing over the next four or five years. It didn't really cross my mind particularly to think of anything beyond that.' In September 1982 he took up the position of junior master for two terms at Collegiate School, Wanganui, on the west coast of New Zealand's North Island. He found it rather dull, and quite soon decided that he wasn't exactly cut out to be a teacher. Even so, his time there cannot have been too bad: he got on very well with the locals, and he enjoyed moderate success as co-writer of a novel about life in a New Zealand boarding school. Looking back, he tends to be philosophical about the whole experience, remarking that he saw it as part of his educational

By the time he reached his twenties, Prince Edward was among the most eligible bachelors in the world. From this photograph of him striking a Victorian stance in Highland evening dress for a charity theatre performance while he was at Cambridge, it is not difficult to see why.

process. There was, however, one thing that he did not learn – how to control his temper with the British press.

Wanganui was the scene of his first outbursts of princely petulance against the press. While there he kept in touch with London via the BBC World Service. And London kept in touch with him. One morning a reporter from the *Daily Mirror* phoned Edward and unexpectedly got straight through. Edward, still very much the prince, was outraged. 'Just what the hell do you think you are doing?' he yelled. 'What on earth gives you the right to call me?' The surprised reporter answered that he wanted to know how he was enjoying his first term as a schoolmaster. 'Well, your curiosity has just killed you . . . in a metaphorical sense,' snapped the Prince. 'This time I won't do what I could do to you. Something rude will happen to you.' If this was not a terribly useful public-relations move by the adolescent prince, it might have been worse – Edward was too polite simply to hang up on the journalist and the conversation continued for half an hour, ending up with a discussion about James Bond films.

While he was down under he went, literally, to the end of the earth to get away from press intrusion, taking a trip he was to describe as 'probably the most memorable week of my life'. In December 1982 he undertook a six-day journey across the frozen landscape of Antarctica. He travelled by toboggan, husky-drawn sledge and helicopter, touring the huts where Captain Scott sheltered in 1902, during his first expedition, and the base camp from which he and his four companions marched off to their deaths in 1912. He stood on the exact point of the South Pole itself, looking north in every direction. He saw icefalls, a 2,000-foot-high frozen waterfall, and a fossilized forest. He joined the Antarctic Ski Club, the most exclusive in the world, and skied in perfect conditions: blue skies, no wind, powder snow, temperature at a perfect 2°C – and no cameras.

As both Prince Charles and Prince Andrew have observed, princes have only a limited number of career options. Traditionally the services have always been the most acceptable choice, and Edward duly made the decision

ABOVE LEFT: *Prince Edward's love-hate relationship with the press began when he was very young indeed, and grew more marked during his time at university. Here he gestures to waiting journalists and cameramen in December 1993, at the time when news of his relationship with Sophie was just breaking. While he appears ruefully good-humoured in this shot, he has on occasion behaved with a very princely arrogance towards newsmen; in a famous incident before he went up to Cambridge, he shouted at a Daily Mirror reporter who telephoned him in New Zealand.*

ABOVE: *Whatever his relations with the media, the Prince knows his duty, and accordingly faces the cameras when it is necessary – in this case wearing a baseball cap to promote a charity devoted to helping London's homeless.*

RIGHT: *Not all Prince Edward's encounters with the media have been combative. He is seen here joking with television presenter Eamonn Holmes on the GMTV programme in January 1993; the Prince used the occasion to launch an initiative aimed at teaching young people new skills.*

ABOVE: *The Prince's interest in the theatre extends beyond acting and producing. Here he visits the Royal Exchange Theatre, Manchester, newly reconstructed after it was destroyed, along with much of the city centre, by an IRA bomb in 1996.*

expected of him. He opted for the Royal Marines – the first member of the royal family to serve in that corps – and it was as a member of the Royal Marines University Cadets Scheme that he arrived at Cambridge in October 1983. The Marines were, in effect, sponsoring his way through college in return for Edward's loyal service with them for a five-year stretch after he had gained his degree. For the time being, however, his only military duties were to spend a few weekends attending training courses at Lympstone in Devon, and to obtain his degree.

Three years is a long time in a young man's life, and Edward was a very different young man when, in 1985, he graduated with a second-class honours degree in history. At the time he said that his three years at Cambridge were the best of his life. University provided him with solitude after the hubbub of public school, and sophistication after years of heartiness. His time was his own, and he was free to develop his own way of life and to learn how to be self-reliant. This was a completely new experience for the cosseted young prince, and sometimes a salutary one, for at university he was no longer the youngest, the quietest or the cleverest, as he had been at home. Moreover, as he by then stood further removed from the line of succession to the throne (by 1984 both Prince Charles's sons had been born), it was most unlikely that he would ever be King; in short, he would always be a prince. One of the many benefits of his time at Cambridge, however, was that he learnt something of the common touch when it came to his peers – by whom he was known simply as Ed – taking his first steps towards becoming an 'ordinary bloke' by appearing as plain Edward Windsor on the university register. Even so, he has always been acutely aware of how his royalness has set him apart. In fact, he can be warmly informal one minute and exasperatingly

royal the next, admitting, in a revealing remark made while he was at Cambridge, 'I may be a human being, but I certainly wouldn't describe myself as being normal. That can never be the case.'

At Cambridge he was determined to stand on his own feet. If he was very careful, he was also very sociable and clearly enjoyed the lifestyle, although unlike many undergraduates, he was not a constant party animal. Besides the social round and, obviously, having to work for his degree, he continued to develop his interests, particularly drama. On the whole he tended to prefer light comedy and revues to more serious fare, and the troupe he was with performed at hospitals, old people's homes and even in pubs. He proved himself to be a wicked mimic with a penchant for slapstick and a considerable sense of fun, which on occasion led him to perform silly stunts such as dancing on the roof of a taxi as it drove through town. In his second year he suffered a bout of glandular fever, and it was while he was laid up that he wrote a children's play, *The Tale of Toothache City*, which he later staged. He also developed his skills as an impresario, a foretaste of his future professional work with his own production company. As he told his biographer, Ingrid Seward, 'I actually began to find that I really enjoyed putting things together and trying to turn what was an idea into a reality.'

Hardly the normal undergraduate, Edward was accompanied everywhere by his two detectives. They rode behind the royal bicycle, attended lectures and refereed college football matches. They also had to deal with the ubiquitous press, who pestered the Prince's fellow undergraduates for information about their royal contemporary. One incident early in Edward's university career so incensed the Master of his college that he felt constrained to complain twice to the Press Council. This came about when a rumour emerged

RIGHT: *At Cambridge, the Prince took his first steps towards becoming an 'ordinary bloke', signing himself in the register as plain Edward Windsor. Although his first love was the theatre, he took part in many of the university's activities, although, unlike many undergraduates, he was not a constant party animal. He remained, too, acutely aware of how his royalness has always set him apart from others, as this shot of him in real-tennis garb in March 1986 hints.*

BELOW: *Prince Edward went up to Jesus College, Cambridge, in October 1983, when he was nineteen. During an official visit to the university the following year, the Queen and the Duke of Edinburgh called upon their youngest son at his college; the Duke is wearing the gown of Chancellor of the University.*

that Edward was having an affair with Corinne Taylor, the leading lady in a production of Arthur Miller's *The Crucible* in which the Prince was a fellow cast member. The paparazzi aimed their lenses at the windows of her bedroom 'just in case something happened.' Nothing ever did. Yet again a formal complaint was fired off when journalists invaded another female student's room, demanding to know where Prince Edward did his laundry. Lucrative offers for royal tittle-tattle were made to several undergraduates, who were well aware that they were under threat of being sent down if any gossip was printed. Luckily everyone closed ranks around the Prince and, despite occasional breaches, his privacy at university was generally respected.

Having always taken life seriously, and having always had to be very careful, it is scarcely surprising that discretion has been an essential ingredient in all Edward's relationships. He knows from bitter experience that romances tend to disintegrate in the heat and glare of the media spotlight. It is perhaps less of a surprise, therefore, than it might otherwise be that Sophie Rhys-Jones was his first girlfriend of any real substance, although that is not to say that he had not had a number of romantic encounters before they first met in 1993. While avoiding a reputation as a royal Casanova, Edward has always had an eye for the girls, and they have swept in and out of his life – some passed muster with his family while others didn't; yet others were unable to stomach the inevitable media feeding frenzy. Until Sophie, none stayed the course.

He met his first girlfriend while he was still a sixth-former. Shelley Whitborn was a horse-mad girl who, in the summer of 1980, nursed Edward's pony, Flash, back to health while working as a trainee groom for Princess Anne at Gatcombe Park. The grateful prince wrote to Shelley from school and the pen pals became close friends, occasionally dating and going to

BELOW: *Edward played rugby for his college while at Cambridge. His closest female friend while at university, Eleanor Weightman, used to watch him playing from the touchline, and he would turn up to watch her play ice hockey. His university rugby career was short-lived, however, as he was victimized on the pitch and constantly besieged by hordes of photographers.*

In sixteenth-century costume during the dress rehearsal for a play.

parties together. Perhaps inevitably, this innocent young love fizzled out as Edward's horizons widened.

Legend has it that two girls competed for the prize of claiming his virginity, which at least goes to prove that this prince is no queen. Was it the maid or was it the model? Neither lasted the course, because in the end neither could resist gossiping. His first experience of sex might therefore have been with a twenty-one-year-old maid at Balmoral when he was eighteen. To his embarrassment, however, she told all the staff about her 'conquest'. Whether her claims were true or not, Edward is extremely sensitive and he will not tolerate anyone who talks.

Some time later an eighteen-year-old model, Romy Adlington, caught his eye at the Royal Yacht Squadron ball during Cowes Week in the summer of 1983. With uncharacteristic assertiveness Edward invited her to join him at Balmoral, only to have her fan the flames of his ardour by turning him down on the grounds that she was booked for various modelling assignments. Edward persisted in the chase until eventually she joined him for an evening at the theatre followed by supper – and then, allegedly, breakfast – at

ABOVE: *At the helm of* The Ashes, *an International Class 3 keelboat, during a race at Cowes in the summer of 1993. The look directed at the photographer says much about Edward's attitude to the press.*

ABOVE RIGHT: *Riding out at the Royal Windsor Horse Show in May 1998. Although not as fine a rider as his sister, Princess Anne, Edward is a very accomplished horseman.*

Buckingham Palace. This relationship set the tone for the Prince's future romances. Romy did the rounds of the royal residences, staying at Windsor, Sandringham and Balmoral, and found the obligatory element of secrecy great fun. She remembers one evening when they went out to dinner, for which Edward elected to wear an elaborate disguise: 'We built up his nose, greased his hair back, added sideburns and stuck on a wonderful moustache. Edward leant forward over the candle and the moustache caught fire. It frazzled away apart from the bit in the middle, which made it look like he was impersonating Adolf Hitler.' Romy adapted well to royal etiquette, and she was probably more popular with the royal family than any of Edward's other girlfriends – until she talked to the tabloids. Before then, however, and to his disappointment, their paths diverged, his to his Cambridge life and hers to a career as an international model and to love in the arms of a new boyfriend.

Most of the girls with whom Prince Edward has become involved either have a healthy love of the outdoors or are connected with the media or the theatre. Spirited and sporty Eleanor Weightman, a fellow undergraduate at Cambridge, became his closest female friend. She would stand on the touch-

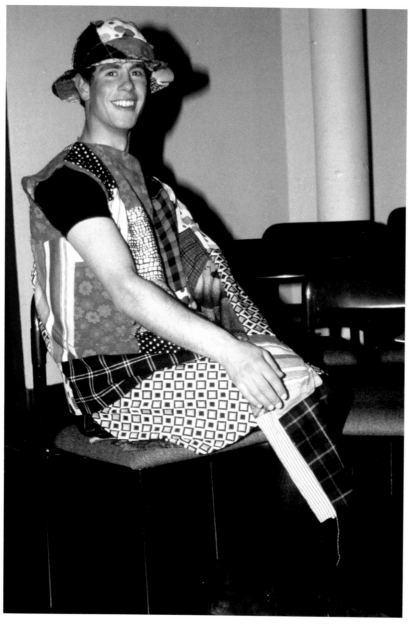

Clown Prince

Drama remained Prince Edward's abiding passion at Cambridge, as it had been at Gordonstoun. He tended to prefer light comedy and revues, and proved himself to be a good mimic with a penchant for slapstick, although he undertook serious roles too.

FACING PAGE: (*top left*) *In costume as Lord Zalburg in the London run of the Cambridge undergraduate revue* Captain Curious and His Incredible Quest, *November 1984; (below left) playing Phon in the same production — the twenty-year-old Prince played eight different parts in the show; (below right) balanced on the shoulders of his detective, Sergeant Andrew Merryless, as the Giant; (top right) during a rehearsal for the Jesus College performance of Arthur Miller's* The Crucible *in November 1983.*

THIS PAGE: *More scenes from* Captain Curious and His Incredible Quest: *(right) as Syd the Spiv, addressing Captain Curious, and (below) posing with the rest of the cast, once more as the evil Lord Zalburg.*

line and watch him play rugby, and he in turn often turned up to watch her play ice hockey. They went skiing together and he stayed at her family home in Cheshire, but as she hated the media attention they drifted apart, although they remain good friends.

Three years later Edward was back in his old stamping ground at Cowes in the Isle of Wight. In 1986, at another Royal Yacht Squadron ball, he met Georgia May. Intelligent, strong-minded, down to earth and fun to be with, she worked as a financial adviser in the City, and probably came closer to marrying him than any other girl until Sophie. She was, too, similar to Sophie in many ways, and notably in looks and temperament. She fitted in well with the royal family and spent weekends with Edward at the royal residences. They kept in touch for two years, with the result that there was much speculation and she was widely tipped as the next royal bride. Georgia, however, who was only twenty-one at the time, became terrified by the appalling media attention when it emerged that her millionaire father was having a gay relationship. This sort of publicity was bad enough for the discreet prince, but when a former boyfriend of Georgia's sold his story to the tabloids her royal relationship was doomed. Edward, along with Georgia and her entire family, was horrified by the clamouring of the press for the most intimate details, and became even more determined to protect any future relationship from this sort of attention.

In September 1986, three months after leaving Cambridge, Edward embarked upon his side of the bargain with the Royal Marines. He cut a dashing figure in the No. 1 dress uniform of an acting lieutenant as best man at his

ABOVE: *'He cut a dashing figure in the No. 1 dress uniform of an acting lieutenant at his brother Andrew's wedding.' The Duke of York and his 'supporter', Prince Edward, riding to Westminster Abbey in the 1902 State Landau on the morning of Andrew's wedding to Sarah Ferguson, 23 July 1986. Prince Andrew wears the ceremonial day dress of a lieutenant, Royal Navy. Five months later Prince Edward resigned from the Royal Marines before completing his training course, an event that received an enormous amount of coverage in the media.*

RIGHT: *The Duke of York, the Princess Royal, Prince Edward and the Princess's husband since 1993, Commander Tim Laurence, RN, clearly amused after a Service of Thanksgiving at St Paul's Cathedral to commemorate the fiftieth anniversary of VE-Day in May 1995.*

ABOVE: *In June 1986 Prince Edward graduated from Cambridge with a second-class honours degree in history.*

brother Andrew's wedding that year, but he was about to enter upon the most traumatic period in his life. Encouraged by his father, who was Captain-General of the Royal Marines, and strengthened by his respect for royal tradition and duty, this adventure had been a boyhood dream for the Prince. He wanted to prove himself, to conform to expectations, and to live up to the achievements of his brothers in the services. In the Royal Navy, Charles earned the nickname 'Action Man', and Andrew had gained hero status as a Sea King helicopter pilot during the Falklands War of 1982. But for some, however well prepared, the tough training in the Marines can be physical and mental torture. His first toughening-up exercise took Edward to the harsh environment of the insect-ridden jungle in Belize, and to a regime of digging trenches and tramping through the dense forest weighed down with weapons and kit. His ordeal continued not just with the continual harsh physical challenges, but with a daily round of humiliation and bullying in front of the other recruits, inflicted by gloating sergeants. It took four miserable months for Edward to decide that he should put personal happiness above duty, and face up to his monumental mistake. Agonizing over his dilemma during the Christmas break, the troubled prince finally broke family ranks and poured out his heart to his former Cambridge tutor, Dr Gavin Mackenzie, who advised him to quit the Marines. At once he found himself bombarded from all sides of the Establishment with the advice that he should persevere. His mind was made up, however, and he stuck by his decision. The news of his intention to resign had been leaked to the press and when he returned to Devon to talk things over with his commanding officer the whole country was

picking over his dilemma; indeed, Dr Mackenzie even featured on the *Jimmy Young Programme* on the radio. Yet despite all the gleeful stories that he was accident prone and a wimp, a *Sunday Express* opinion poll accorded him an 80 per cent approval rating. Perhaps the public recognized that it was strength, not weakness, that sustained him in questioning the value of a military career, and in turning his back on tradition to choose his own way forward.

There was, however, an even worse public-relations fiasco awaiting the Prince, even as he prepared eagerly for life outside the services. Throughout his life Edward has been plagued by 'dentopedalogy', a term coined by Prince Philip, a fellow sufferer, to define the unfortunate habit of opening one's mouth and putting one's foot in it. Now the affliction was about to strike him again, as his juvenile enthusiasm and lack of savvy landed him in a mess that made a much more lasting impression on the public than his Royal Marines débâcle. Before disaster overwhelmed it, Edward's new enterprise had seemed to have everything going for it, and it has to be said that some good came of it, not the least being that he raised over a million pounds for charity, he gained his first taste of television production, and he met his future partner, Malcolm Cockren. And yet all this was completely overshadowed by the spectacle of the Prince making a right royal fool of himself.

What happened was this. Prince Edward had for many years been a fan of the BBC Television programme *It's A Knock-Out*, a family party-game show featuring the silliest jousts and japes imaginable. Edward devised The Grand Charity Knockout Tournament based on this format, and roped in an amazing cast of fifty international stars, as well as royal relations in the persons of his brother, Prince Andrew, and his wife Sarah, and his sister, Princess Anne. Deploying his considerable organizational skills, he co-ordinated the event down to almost the last detail, from sponsorship and costumes to camera angles. His own yellow Tudor-style costume, set off with a plumed hat and yellow tights, prompted *The Times* to describe him as 'one of Shakespeare's lesser jesters', and he has displayed a horror of being photographed in fancy dress ever since. Even so, the silly antics that took place at Alton Towers on

ABOVE LEFT: *Although he left the Marines without taking up his commission, Prince Edward shares with the rest of his family a gift for getting on well with servicemen. Here he talks to Pensioners of the Royal Hospital, Chelsea, during the annual Founder's Day celebration. The Prince wears oak leaves in honour of the Hospital's founder, Charles II, who, after the Royalist defeat at Worcester in 1651, took refuge from his pursuers in an oak tree.*

ABOVE: *Prince Edward, in the uniform of an acting lieutenant, Royal Marines, with his grandmother at a commemoration service in Westminster Abbey to mark the fortieth anniversary of VE-Day, 10 May 1985. Behind them stands Princess Alice, Duchess of Gloucester, Edward's great-aunt, who was born a year after the Queen Mother.*

RIGHT: *The eighteen-year-old Prince Edward on the Royal Marines assault course at the Corps's training camp at Lympstone, Devon, during a three-day assessment course in May 1982. The Prince was, and remains, the first member of the royal family to opt for a commission in the Marines, both his brothers, like their father, being naval officers.*

that rainy day in June 1987 might have been long forgotten, had Edward not let loose another of his petulant outbursts. That this was again directed at the press only made matters worse, and ensured his complete humiliation.

For the one element to which Edward had not paid sufficient attention was the one he most needed if the event was to be a success – the media. He had the press cooped up in a wet enclosure without a bar and refused to allow them to take any photographs. As a result, having spent a miserable day they missed their deadlines, and began to feel a huge resentment against Prince Edward and the way in which he had treated them. Naively, he had expected their support for his charitable efforts, but when he made his appearance before the disgruntled journalists after the show, not one of them had any compliments for the buffoonery of the day, which in any case they had not been able to witness. For his part, he was mortified at their lack of enthusiasm, and infuriated by their derision when he asked them if they had enjoyed what they had seen. Now, at last, the press got a story. Having made a number of graceless comments, the peeved prince stormed out of the press tent. Inevitably his undignified tantrum made the front pages the next morning –

'IT'S A WALK-OUT' being just one of several such headlines. The journalists were furious to have spent all day trying to cover a charity event only to be 'sneered at by a rudely offensive young man,' as Linda Lee Potter wrote in the *Daily Mail*. It was a disastrous day for Edward's public image and one that he is still sensitive about. He has always been ambitious, but he also craves praise. He was left to put the whole unhappy business down to bitter experience, and to focus on the million pounds he had raised for charity. Even that, however, could not alter the fact that the painfully embarrassing spectacle of four senior members of the royal family disporting themselves in this way – and in silly costumes, to boot – had a profound, and perhaps lastingly damaging effect, upon the public's perception of the whole institution of the monarchy.

In the event, a blind date for the Prince with the girl of many men's fantasies made an excellent diversion for the press. One of Edward's closest friends, James Baker, son of broadcaster Richard Baker, was working at TV-am in 1987. That summer he invited a newly joined secretary named Ulrika Jonsson to accompany him to the Henley Regatta ball. In her borrowed ball gown, she was somewhat flabbergasted to drive via Windsor Castle for a few glasses of Pimm's on the lawn with what turned out to be her royal partner for the evening, Prince Edward. After that they went on several dates together, and formed a friendship that was to suit the purposes of both of them. Ulrika was the first girl Edward had been seen with in public, and the publicity did her career no harm at all. (She also recited publicly the now familiar mantra, repeated by Sophie, 'I can tell you he's not gay.') In fact, if Edward had been serious about Ulrika he would have kept the relationship entirely under wraps. Instead, he seemed to gain a taste for fooling the press, for he devised another smokescreen appearance, happily allowing himself to be photographed with Anastasia Cooke, James Baker's girlfriend, now his wife, as a bluff for the journalists. By contrast, it is notable that he allowed only a handful of photo opportunities of himself with Sophie during the nearly six years of their courtship.

ABOVE: *Edward's name was also linked with that of the talented British actress and singer Ruthie Henshall, the star of a number of successful West End musicals, whom he dated for some time in the late 1980s; she remains a good friend of both the Prince and Sophie.*

LEFT: *Prince Edward with his future employer, Andrew Lloyd Webber, and the composer's then wife, Sarah Brightman, in June 1986. Just under two years later the Prince went to work for Lloyd Webber and his Really Useful Theatre Group.*

RIGHT: *When it came to girlfriends, he seemed to enjoy trying to fool the press, allowing himself to be photographed with the television journalist Anastasia Cooke, the girlfriend of one of his closest friends, James Baker, son of the broadcaster Richard Baker. The couple married in 1994, although the Prince's ruse did not stop journalists from linking his name with Anastasia's, claiming that the 'romance' had ended because she wished to pursue her broadcasting career.*

Edward was linked to several girls during his theatre days, of whom the most celebrated was the talented and successful musical star, Ruthie Henshall. They met when she was in *Cats*, and she remains a good friend of both him and Sophie. Edward admired her tremendously and she was a regular guest at Buckingham Palace and Sandringham for a while, and even poignantly sang the classic Judy Garland song 'You Made Me Love You' for him at his twenty-fifth birthday party in March 1989. He thoughtfully stayed away from her first night in *Crazy For You* so as not to steal her thunder, the sort of consideration that prompts her to say of him, 'Edward's a jolly nice guy. He's a friend and he just happens to be royal.'

RIGHT: *The Queen and Prince Philip are greeted by their youngest son upon their arrival at the Royal Festival Hall, London, for a concert, organized by Prince Edward, to mark their golden wedding anniversary in 1997.*

FAR RIGHT: *Promoting British art and culture at a luncheon to mark 'Festival UK98' at the British Embassy in Tokyo, 22 January 1998. The event was part of the year-long festival, held throughout Japan, aimed at raising Britain's profile there.*

Having given up a military career, and with the 'Royal Knockout' disaster behind him, it was time for Edward to get on with the career he had set his heart on. First, however, he had to get through the stage door. He had become much wiser and more self-reliant after taking his own decision to leave the Marines, and as a result had a better idea of what he could do and how to set about doing it. He decided to apply to Andrew (now Lord) Lloyd Webber's Really Useful Theatre Group for a job – not in fact to work alongside the great man himself, but to learn the business by starting on the lowest rung of the organization, and in the event he was taken on for just such a post.

FACING PAGE ABOVE: *Prince Edward chats to members of the cast of Andrew Lloyd Webber's hit musical* Starlight Express, *then in its twelfth anniversary, on the occasion of its 5,000th performance in March 1996.*

FACING PAGE BELOW: *Speaking in January 1998 to the press at the launch of* Crown and Country, *a series of twenty-four half-hour TV documentaries narrated by himself and produced by his own company, Ardent Productions, which he founded with two partners in 1993. The programmes were shown on the History Channel, and illustrated the influence of kings and queens upon the buildings and landscapes of Britain. A good deal of the credit for Ardent's success, after a shaky start, belongs to Prince Edward.*

LEFT: *Arriving for his first day of work with Lloyd Webber's company in February 1988. The fact that the Prince was carrying a box of tea bags says much about his self-deprecating sense of humour in response to press gibes about his new job as a 'royal tea boy'. In fact, he started as a production assistant, but his skills were soon recognized when he was promoted.*

Prince Edward is the first of the Queen's children to be an employee. By the time he started his job he was certainly tough enough to deal good-humouredly with all the 'royal tea boy' gibes, the inevitable result of the fact that on his first day at work in February 1988 he arrived brandishing a packet of tea bags. At work he revelled in his first taste of freedom as plain Edward Windsor, as he did too in the nickname 'Babs', after the actress Barbara Windsor. But although no one took any notice of him as he mingled with the crowds in Soho, he could never quite forget his royal status with his detective always standing by, even when he put the kettle on. When asked by journalist Alice de Smith, 'Given the chance and if you weren't a prince of the Realm, would you become an actor?' he replied without any hesitation, 'Yes I would.' He is said to have turned down offers to appear in *Dr Who* and *Bread*, and another to play the part of Buttons in a Christmas pantomime. Since he is a prince of the Realm, however, his next best ambition was to become a theatre producer.

At work his administrative and organizational skills were soon noticed. Lloyd Webber promoted him to Overseas Co-ordinator, and among many foreign productions he helped to get *Aspects of Love* ready for Broadway. Then, after two years with Really Useful, he left, along with five colleagues, to join Lloyd Webber's producer, Biddy Haywood, in her new venture, Theatre Division. His new job was as Technical Director. As it turned out this was not the wisest move during a recession, and after two unsuccessful West End productions the company folded in 1991. Edward was twenty-seven, unemployed, and had an annual Civil List allowance of £100,000 that was about to be abolished. It took him just six months to get his act together.

Ignoring the advice of his father to take up a sensible job in accountancy or management training, much safer options than the high-risk television industry, he stuck to his guns and opted for the latter. With partner Malcolm Cockren, whom he had met during the 'Royal Knockout' venture, and an old friend, Eben Foggitt, Edward put all his enthusiasm, ideas and organizational ability into setting up Ardent Productions in 1993. Cockren had advised him that television production would be less risky than the theatre, Edward's first love. He refused to allow himself to be financially protected in any way, raised company funding himself and, making use of his natural flair for business and figures, even wrote his own business plan. He wanted to be judged on what he could achieve, rather than by who he is; furthermore, he believes that being a prince is in fact a hindrance, because he has had to prove himself a hundred times over.

He started with noble intentions, notably when he gave his view that 'making a royal programme would give the wrong impression. I don't want to trade on that association any more than I intend trading on my title.' Before long, however, Channel Four had commissioned a three-part documentary series on Edward's favourite sport of real tennis. A more ambitious drama series, *Annie's Bar*, proved to be a competent satirical soap, but it failed to capture the viewers' imagination and a further series was not produced. Ardent's turning point came, however, when Edward broke his own first rule of engagement with a documentary about his great-uncle, King Edward VIII. Entitled *Edward on Edward* and presented by himself, it was a well-made programme and a poised and charismatic performance. The subject matter was

ABOVE: *On 20 December 1993, three months after his first meeting with Sophie, the Prince sent an open letter to editors, denying rumours that he and his latest girlfriend were to marry and asking that they be spared the attentions of journalists and photographers.*

FAR LEFT: *Prince Edward laughing with Diana, Princess of Wales, at a Commonwealth Day reception at Marlborough House in March 1993.*

LEFT: *First day as joint managing director of Ardent Productions Ltd, December 1993 – Edward waves to well-wishers as he arrives at the company's offices in Central London.*

RIGHT: *The Queen looks on as Mary Robinson, former President of the Republic of Ireland, now the United Nations High Commissioner for Human Rights, receives a warm greeting from Prince Edward at Buckingham Palace.*

BELOW: *That Sophie's acceptance by Edward's family has long been complete could not be better demonstrated than by this photograph of her sitting with him, his mother, father, brothers and sister during the paying-off ceremony for the Royal Yacht* Britannia *in Portsmouth in November 1997.*

very topical at the time, since it covered the controversial decision not to award the title of honour 'Her Royal Highness' to the Duchess of Windsor, the woman for whose love Edward VIII had abdicated in 1936, while debate was raging over the same treatment of both the Princess of Wales and the Duchess of York following their separations from Prince Charles and Prince Andrew. The American network, CBS, were impressed enough to sign an eight-programme deal with Ardent, worth an estimated £2 million. The Prince was vindicated at last.

He also hit the right note with his documentary *Windsor Restored*, which chronicled the reconstruction and restoration of Windsor Castle after the devastating fire of 1992. 'I thought it was too good a story to miss,' he said, 'not only because of the number of people involved in the restoration, but because of the anecdotes. I thought it would make great television.' And so it did – not least for scenes like that when, at the end of the restoration, some 1,500 craftsmen celebrated their efforts with the Queen over beer and pizza. Today Ardent Productions has turned the corner and has a busy production schedule, currently developing a major costume-drama series based on the popular Inspector Pitt novels of Anne Perry. A good deal of the credit for the company's success undoubtedly belongs to Prince Edward.

In December 1993, after Edward and Sophie's fateful meeting on the real-tennis court that September, Edward issued his unprecedented open letter to the press denying that they had any plans to marry and asking them to stay away; 'I am very conscious that other members of my immediate family have been subjected to similar attention and it has not been at all beneficial to their relationships,' he said. He was determined to protect this relationship, painfully aware of the traumatic events taking place in the marriages of his two brothers, events that were tarnishing the reputation of the royal family. Although by nature he is shy, he seemed to blossom in Sophie's company. He was clearly captivated but, ever cautious, did not rush in. This is clear from the length of their courtship, something that has given them time to establish their careers and to deal with the endless rounds of media speculation. They are only too aware of expectations for their marriage, and of its importance to the stability of the monarchy.

ABOVE LEFT: *On 31 August 1997, with shocking suddenness, Diana, Princess of Wales, was killed in a car crash in Paris. The effect upon the British public and throughout the rest of the world, as well as upon the royal family, was profound. Princess Anne, her husband, Commander Timothy Laurence, her son, Peter Phillips, and Prince Edward leaving Westminster Abbey after the Princess's funeral on 6 September 1997. This national tragedy was not the least of the factors that helped to delay Edward's announcement of his engagement, since it would have been inappropriate, at best, to have made any wedding announcement until after a decent interval of time had elapsed.*

ABOVE : *The Prince of Wales's elder son, Prince William, talks to his uncle outside Clarence House on the occasion of the Queen Mother's ninety-eighth birthday in August 1998. This photograph was taken some three weeks before the first anniversary of the death of Prince William's mother.*

Bagshot Park in Surrey, which Prince Edward has leased from the Crown Estate since 1997, and where the couple will live after they are married. The large Victorian mansion, with its outbuildings and extensive grounds, is also now the headquarters of the Prince's company, Ardent Productions.

In 1997 Prince Edward took a fifty-year lease from the Crown Estate and moved in to Bagshot Park, a Victorian mansion in Surrey set in nearly sixty acres of grounds. At the time he persisted in denying rumours of marriage, saying, 'Please do not read too much into this.' In fact, it will be his and Sophie's marital home. In June 1998 he moved Ardent's production offices from a cramped office in Soho to the Old Stables at Bagshot Park.

Prince Edward is his own man, and one who has shown great strength of character in making a success of life outside the royal circle. His — by royal standards, at least — unconventional choices have marked him as a true product of his times. Not without controversy, and after considerable effort and much persistence, he has overcome the constraints of his background to find his true vocation. Today, with great self-assurance, he leads a near-normal life, building a career while at the same time attending to his official duties. Now, with Sophie at his side, he has come as close as he can to his boyhood dream.

'I don't think it would have been right before, and I don't think she would have said yes' — Prince Edward and his fiancée on the day their engagement was announced, 6 January 1999.

❧ The Bride ❧

SOPHIE is a thoroughly modern royal bride, a multi-faceted character with her own ideas and ambitions. Her relationship with Prince Edward is not simply some fairy-tale romance, owing more to fiction than to reality — instead, it is a love match between the public-relations consultant and the television production executive.

It is nearly six years since her chance first meeting with Prince Edward. Since then she has made a dignified and gradual entrance on to the world stage. She is also well rehearsed in coping with constant press attention and speculation, and with the pressure of public expectations for this marriage. As she herself has commented, 'I am ready for it now and I am fully aware of the responsibilities and commitments.' True to character she plans to continue with her job — 'Yes, it will be very much business as usual.' Clear-headed and hard-working, Sophie is chairwoman and co-owner of R-JH, the public-relations company she helped to found, and has an impressive portfolio of high-profile, blue-chip clients.

She has her own mind and has independently built her own extremely successful career. The media advice she gives her clients she can now put to good use on her own behalf as she takes up her new role in Britain's first family. She is, too, perhaps rather better equipped to second-guess what may happen than previous royal ingénues. Given her blonde good looks, elegance and sense of style, she will inevitably be compared with the late Diana, Princess of Wales, but it is a comparison she is known to dread. Unlike Diana, Sophie has the advantage of a stable family background, rooted in a comfortable, middle-class, Home Counties upbringing. She is the first real outsider to enter the inner sanctum of the House of Windsor. Unlike all the others who have

FACING PAGE: *Sophie — an unpublished photograph taken before the engagement. Inevitably her blonde good looks have led to comparisons with the late Diana, Princess of Wales, but in fact the two women could scarcely have been more different in character and outlook.*

BELOW: *Prince Edward and Sophie Rhys-Jones leave Buckingham Palace on their way to St James's Palace to announce their engagement, 6 January 1999. Nowadays, Sophie gets to ride in the front and the detective in the back, but in the early days she sat behind, with the detective next to Edward.*

LEFT: *The nineteen-year-old Lady Diana Spencer reacts with shock as she arrives back at her London flat — to find that the linking of her name romantically with that of the Prince of Wales has made her a target for every newshound in the capital.*

LEFT: *The nineteen-year-old Lady Diana Spencer reacts with shock as she arrives back at her London flat — to find that the linking of her name romantically with that of the Prince of Wales has made her a target for every newshound in the capital.*

BELOW LEFT: *Sophie Rhys-Jones is caught by photographers as she prepares to drive home from work; after the announcement of her engagement to Prince Edward, she too was rarely without attendant journalists and photographers.*

RIGHT: *Sophie arriving at Heathrow Airport after flying from Aberdeen with Prince Edward. They had spent a weekend with the Queen at Balmoral.*

BELOW: *The tabloids remain intrigued by Sophie's passing resemblance to the late Princess of Wales. When this photograph was taken in July 1994 the Princess still dominated headlines, and so comparisons were inevitable.*

married the Queen's children, Sophie has had no previous connections with the royal household. For despite her double-barrelled surname, she is no aristocrat, although she can trace her family back to show that she is a sixth cousin once removed of Viscount Molesworth, who is in turn remotely

BELOW: *This photograph illustrates clearly how quickly Prince Edward's family took his new girlfriend to their hearts, as she travels in a car with Princess Anne, her husband and son.*

related to the royal family. Thus she may be an outsider, but she is not quite a commoner.

Sophie's wardrobe reflects her busy working and social life. She was not brought up as a clothes horse, but she undoubtedly has an eye for style, elegantly matching modern classic suits with fine jewellery and spangled details. When she first met the Prince her clothes mostly came from high-street stores. In those days she was able to make sartorial mistakes in relative obscurity, and the Queen is said to have observed approvingly, 'You wouldn't notice her in a crowd'. Now that she holds centre stage, she is a regular client of several trusty Sloane Street designers such as Amanda Wakeley and Tomasz Starzewski. With her strong bone structure she is able to carry off dramatic hats and structured suits, often adding playful touches of theatrical detail. She has the gift, too, of looking equally chic in sports clothes or wax jacket and green wellies. This is not perhaps surprising – off duty, Sophie is a keen and fearless sportswoman, qualities that have also helped to endear her to the royal family. Her first love is skiing, she is a good shot and she shares the royal passion for riding. She has, moreover, the old-fashioned sporting spirit, meaning that she will try – and has tried – almost anything, from windsurfing and scuba diving to bungee jumping.

Even before her engagement Sophie seemed to have the Queen's approval. She has been a regular guest at the most private of royal-family events, and is well aware of royal etiquette and protocol, which she deals with easily and gracefully. She has spent many weekends at Windsor Castle as well as holidays at Sandringham, Balmoral and aboard *Britannia*, before the Royal Yacht left the Queen's service. Such hospitality would have been unthinkable a few years earlier. After the break-up of her other children's marriages the Queen was

keen that Prince Edward's relationship with Sophie should be allowed to move at its own pace without the restrictions of old-fashioned customs. One result of this is that Sophie has her own set of rooms at Buckingham Palace, close to Prince Edward's, although, as she has said, 'Contrary to popular opinion, we have never lived together, and I have never issued any ultimatums.'

Friends describe Sophie as gregarious, vivacious and straightforward, completely lacking in pretension and with a good sense of humour which she is said to share with the Queen. She is fortunate to have had many wonderful experiences before she met Prince Edward, not least because her worldliness marks a great contrast to the backgrounds of Lady Diana Spencer and Sarah Ferguson before their marriages. Her travels and adventures in Australia and Europe do reveal, however, the two contrasting aspects of Sophie. Professionally she is sober, level-headed, cool and rather distant. Personally she is enthusiastic, impulsive, and flighty, and she has had to learn to rein in

Sophie's Style

BELOW LEFT: *A businesslike Sophie, managing to look both smart and casual, on her way to another appointment in August 1995.*

BELOW: *After the engagement — Sophie smiles at photographers as she arrives for a party at the Natural History Museum in London. Her long experience of public-relations work has made her adept at dealing with the press.*

her spontaneity when dealing with the somewhat starchy formality of royal circles. She also has a short temper, usually displayed when things don't go her way, something that she cheekily blames on her mother's Irish ancestry.

Despite the couple's close professional links with the media, they both prefer their private lives to remain just that — private. Prince Edward's relaxed courtship, and the warm welcome accorded Sophie by his family, have already provided her with firm support amid the undoubted stresses of becoming a modern royal bride.

Sophie Helen Rhys-Jones was born on 20 January 1965, ten months after Prince Edward. Her father, Christopher, was born in Borneo, the son of a schoolmaster, Theo Rhys-Jones. After an adventurous colonial life, the family returned to England in the mid-1930s to live in the West Country. During his late teens Christopher tried his hand at teaching, but after a while he gave it

BELOW: *In the Royal Enclosure at Ascot, the hat eye-catching and stylish, without being — as so many — outrageously silly.*

BELOW RIGHT: *Watching Prince Charles playing in a polo match at Cirencester in 1997.*

up to follow his instincts for travelling and set off for the wide open spaces of Africa; like his daughter, he is a natural outdoor type, something reflected in his lifelong love of shooting, fishing and sailing. During Christopher's globe-trotting days he met Kensington-based secretary Mary O'Sullivan in Gibraltar. They married in Westminster and settled into a life of modest comfort in Oxfordshire. Their first child, David – now an insurance executive and racing commentator – was born in 1963, and Sophie arrived two years later. She is on the cusp of Capricorn and Aquarius, star signs associated with qualities of prudence, offbeat humour, self-discipline and, perhaps significantly, a willingness to postpone romantic attachments until a career has been established.

Not long after Sophie's birth the Rhys-Jones family moved to a detached Victorian farmhouse in Brenchley, Kent, the village where they still live today. Her father, now retired, worked in the motor trade and became a manager for the London Chemical Company selling, among other products, car tyres. Her mother worked locally as a secretary taking home typing at £3 per hour to bolster the family income.

Sophie's first love was ballet, and as a girl she yearned to be a professional ballerina. As it happened, she had family connections with the world of the theatre, her chief inspiration coming from her uncle, Thane Bettany, and aunt, Anne Kettle, who were both members of the Royal Ballet. She loved visiting Covent Garden and Sadlers Wells, as she still does. With the family tradition to uphold, she started taking ballet lessons from the tender age of four, and danced regularly until she was seventeen, reaching Grade 4 in ballet and dance. Every week without fail she attended ballet classes in Brenchley, and

Sophie (looking over the shoulders of the girls second and third from left in the front row) at school – a good all-rounder, 'her strengths lay in pursuits that demanded self-expression', something that explains her long-established love for ballet and acting.

she always performed in the summer shows at the annual fête in nearby Paddock Wood. Her regular dance partner and best friend in those idyllic days was Sarah Sienesi, who became her first flatmate in London and is now a stalwart companion in her present role in the royal limelight.

Like her elder brother David she went to Dulwich College Preparatory School in Cranbrook, Kent, a boarding school which she attended as a day girl. She proved herself a good all-rounder with something of a tomboy

ABOVE: *The sign on the approach to Brenchley in Kent, the village to which Sophie's parents moved not long after her birth, and where they still live.*

RIGHT: *Sophie's parents, Christopher and Mary Rhys-Jones, photographed at the time of their daughter's engagement. Sophie inherited her love of adventure, travel and the outdoors from her father; cheekily, she claims her short temper is a legacy of her mother's Irish ancestry.*

Sophie (far left) with a group of friends during her days at West Kent College, which she began to attend in 1982, when she was seventeen.

streak, which came to the fore when she took boxing lessons from the unlikely figure of the school chaplain. Her headmaster, Robin Preverett, OBE, recalls, 'My memory of her is very much of a happy, popular, natural girl with lots of common sense'.

From Dulwich she passed the entry exams for Kent College School for Girls in Pembury, where her sporting prowess soon became evident. Besides her ballet, she was an active member of the netball, hockey, athletics and swimming teams. Her strengths lay in pursuits that demanded self-expression, although she continued to be a good all-rounder. Academically her strongest subject was English, and it is an enduring regret of hers that she didn't study harder so that she could read English at university. 'If I had my time again I would have gone to university,' she says. Even so she gained six O levels and, later, an A level in English, as well as another O level in law.

However much she might have enjoyed her schooldays, she was at the same time conscious of the financial burden the fee-paying school put on her parents. While her father paid for David's place at Wellington College in Somerset, it was the money her mother earned that put Sophie through school. To ease the strain on her parents, she therefore decided to assume responsibility for the next stage of her education. In 1982 she won a place at the West Kent College of Further Education in Tonbridge, where she took an A level in English, an O level in law, and a secretarial course. The latter, which

The teenaged Sophie enjoys an evening in the local pub.

at least earned her another qualification, was not a particularly vocational choice; it was 'just for something to do,' she said. While at college she also earned some extra cash by working as a part-time waitress in a local pub, the Halfway House.

With her best friend Sarah, the teenaged Sophie joined the Cranbrook Operatic Society. Before she could do so, however, she had to pass the audition, which meant singing solo in front of a critical producer; 'It was,' she remembers, 'the worst moment of my life,' for although her acting and dancing were strong, her voice was rather shaky. Much to her surprise, though, she was offered a part in the chorus of *My Fair Lady*, during which her dancing abilities came to the fore as she ran through the intricacies of various routines with other members of the cast.

The truth is that Sophie, like Prince Edward, had from an early age been seduced by the allure of the stage. Her first part, as the cockerel in *The Wizard of Oz* for the local amateur dramatic society, was hardly the stuff of great acting, but she loved the smell of greasepaint all the same. There were, too, other compensations for the budding thespian. Again with her friend Sarah Sienesi, she attended theatre workshops at the nearby Tonbridge Boys' School, and it was there that she met her first serious boyfriend, a dashing sixth-former named David Kinder. He too was passionate about the theatre, a quality Sophie seems to admire in her men, later graduating to parts in *Dr Who* and

ABOVE: *The Rhys-Jones's house in Brenchley. Sophie lived in the village from infancy until she left to work in London in July 1984, when she was nineteen.*

Grange Hill before abandoning acting to take up teaching. Although the romance was short lived they have remained friends, and over the years Sophie has been a regular visitor to the Kinder family home in Chislehurst, Kent, while she remembers with affection the summer tennis and cricket parties hosted by David's parents.

In fact, it can be said that all Sophie's former boyfriends have been thoroughly decent chaps, and she has remained firm friends with most of them. Indeed, she was introduced to her favourite sport, skiing, thanks to the generosity of a former teenage boyfriend, John Blackman. For Sophie's twenty-first birthday present, John clubbed together with a group of friends to pay for a skiing holiday to celebrate her coming of age. She has skied with John and his family regularly since that time, and he is still one of her closest friends.

Sophie lodged with John's parents when in July 1984, aged nineteen, she moved to London to take up her first job with the Quentin Bell public relations organization, where for six months she was secretary to the managing director. She moved from there to take up a similar post working for the Tim Arnold sales promotion agency, which she left just over a year later for a potentially more glamorous job working with the publicity manager of Capital Radio. There she organized press launches and photo calls for the national and local media, and wrote endless press releases. It was mundane at first but it was fun, if hardly glamorous, as was perhaps typified by the highlight of the year when she attended the grand opening of the M25 motorway.

FACING PAGE: *The Halfway House in Brenchley, where Sophie worked as a part-time waitress while she was at West Kent College in the early 1980s.*

Sophie at Work

A series of exclusive photographs, never published before, of Sophie Rhys-Jones working on a PR campaign in 1994. Unposed, and often taken when she was unaware of being photographed, they capture her decisiveness, her professionalism, and her easy charm — as well as her ability to look as chic in a waxed jacket . . .

Girl about Town

. . . as she does elegant in evening dress at a Royal Gala concert at the Festival Hall in London; or stylish as she arrives for work at her Mayfair offices; or streetwise as she heads home after a shopping trip.

She quickly settled into London life as a typical girl-about-town and enjoyed several relationships, none of them particularly serious. For a time she went out with a Royal Engineers captain and then with her father's godson, Rupert Keane, who is now married and living near Prince Charles in Tetbury, Gloucestershire, and with whom, as with many of her old flames, she still keeps in touch. She also kept in touch with many of her old friends from school days, went to the Dance Attic in Putney and often spent evenings in various 'Sloane-Ranger' haunts around Chelsea and Fulham. She turned many heads as she bombed round town in her classic Morris Minor, given to her by her then boyfriend, Jeremy Barkley, eleven years her senior. She was with Jeremy, albeit more off than on, for nearly two years and – as seems to be almost the norm with Sophie – they are still friends. 'She was and is a lovely girl and we had a lot of fun together,' he remembers.

In May 1987 Sophie moved to Capital Radio's promotions department, something that proved to be a turning point for the twenty-two-year-old. The

department was run by Anita Hamilton and the two became close friends, and still meet regularly for a drink and a gossip. In her new job Sophie organized publicity and outside events, regularly travelling with the station DJs and backup staff when Capital went on the road. Feisty, spontaneous, gregarious and at times quietly flirtatious, she is remembered with affection by station staff and DJs. Programme Controller Pete Simmons remembers that 'She got on with everyone and we all adored her. She was always game for a laugh.' Such was their loyalty that as soon as her royal romance was revealed, a bawdy, although completely innocent, photograph of Sophie fooling around for the camera with breakfast show DJ Chris Tarrant was removed from the office wall in great haste. Sophie and Chris have remained excellent friends, something helped by the fact that she also gets on particularly well with his wife Ingrid.

Sophie loved her days at Capital – the station now refers to her as 'our Sophie' – but after five years of London life she wanted a change. While her

PR girl — Sophie with Lady Cobham, launching the First Steps Appeal charity for small children in Birmingham, September 1995. She was then still working for MCM, the PR company she had been with when she first met Prince Edward two years earlier.

wanderlust was never quite as strong as her father's, she decided that she'd like to see more of the world. In the winter of 1989, therefore, she headed for the Alps, having joined Bladon Lines, a ski company catering largely for the Sloane-Ranger end of the market, as a representative in the picturesque Swiss resort of Crans-Montana. Between her many duties of greeting guests at Zurich airport, keeping an eye on six chalet girls plus up to thirty-six guests, throwing fondue parties and overseeing the accounts, she brushed up her ski-ing technique and learned to snowboard. She also fell head over heels in love with Michael O'Neill, a rugged Australian ski instructor. It was, she admitted afterwards, her first true love affair. They enjoyed a steady relationship throughout the four-month season and afterwards she flew with him to Australia, entranced by his yarns of barbecues, surfing, sunshine and the easy-going lifestyle down under. But although she stayed in the country for over a year, her romance with Michael foundered after just eight weeks. As luck would have it, however, an old friend from London, Andrew Cullity, arrived on the scene to save this damsel in distress. He was working in Sydney for an international courier company and managed to wangle Sophie a job working for a rival shipping firm.

Sophie's new role as Girl Friday was very monotonous, mainly consisting of chasing missing packages and book-keeping, but it helped pay the rent at the house she shared with Andrew in the fashionable Paddington district of Sydney. Moreover, while work was somewhat dull, her social life was hectic, and the carefree lifestyle suited Sophie's energetic and sporty temperament. Days were spent at Bondi Beach improving her surfing and topping up her tan, and nights carousing around the cafés and restaurants of one of the world's loveliest cities. Her sense of fun made her many friends and admirers, and, ever the daredevil, she even tried bungee jumping, at a time when the sport was still relatively uncommon. 'It was such a thrill, I've never felt anything like it,' she says, reliving the moment when she hurtled towards the water hundreds of feet below.

Her adventurous instincts prompted her to quit her job and go backpacking around the Australian outback. For much of her three-month tour she travelled solo, a sure sign of a very independent and self-reliant young woman, although she did team up for a time with a Scottish girl, Lynne Muir, who was on her own round-the-world trek. Sophie also went cruising on a luxury yacht off the Australian coast and learned to scuba dive with the

In March 1996 Sophie helped to launch National Mother and Baby Week in aid of the Baby Lifeline charity, a favourite cause of hers, and for which she handled the PR account. Here she poses with former Rolling Stone Bill Wyman and his daughter Katharine at the launch of the event.

Faces of Sophie

FACING PAGE ABOVE: *At a charity real-tennis tournament in which Prince Edward was playing in February 1994, five months after they first met.*

FACING PAGE BELOW LEFT: *Arriving, just after Prince Edward, for a production of* The Threepenny Opera *by Bertolt Brecht at the Lyric Theatre, Hammersmith.*

FACING PAGE BELOW RIGHT: *At Heathrow Airport to catch a flight, with the Prince, for Scotland.*

RIGHT: *At the launch of Britain's first Haven Trust Centre in London. Her company handles the public relations for the charity.*

BELOW: *Arriving for work on her thirtieth birthday, 20 January 1995.*

BELOW RIGHT: *Leaving the offices of PR company MCM in Hammersmith on the day Prince Edward sent his letter to editors asking that both he and, in particular, Sophie be spared the attentions of the press.*

graphic designer, seafarer and telltale Eon Balmain. He was infatuated by Sophie, although he never quite succeeded in sweeping her off her feet, however hard he tried. He admitted that 'She had something about her that made you look twice. She was very attractive.' He also remembers that she was very discreet about her past, always retaining an air of mystery, never discussing past or present lovers. In marked contrast to her behaviour, he later spilt the beans about their friendship to the tabloids.

In June 1991 Sophie came home. She had been away for a year and missed her family, but most importantly she wanted to be back in time for her father's sixtieth birthday. Back in Britain a new romance took her to new heights – literally, for her new boyfriend, dentist Tim King, was a fanatical amateur pilot. Sophie's love of thrills and spills was tested to the limit the first time Tim took her for a spin, for his aircraft developed a fault at 1,000 feet and they were forced to make an emergency landing; fortunately both the occupants and the plane were shaken but not hurt. He and Sophie would fly across the Channel to Le Touquet just for a night out, although these jaunts continued to have their element of risk. On one occasion they flew down to Andorra for a few days' skiing and had to make an emergency landing at Bordeaux due to bad weather, bringing the whole airport to a standstill. There are no lasting hard feelings – Tim still looks after Sophie's teeth!

FACING PAGE ABOVE: *Sophie at a press launch in April 1998 – by then she had left MCM and set up R-JH, a public-relations company she runs with a partner, Murray Harkin.*

FACING PAGE BELOW: *Judy Ledger, founder of the charity Baby Lifeline, with her two children and Sophie. Of all her clients at MCM, Sophie found the charity's account the most rewarding.*

BELOW: *Working in public relations, as well as having the Queen's youngest son for a boyfriend, has left Sophie well accustomed to the lifestyles of the rich and famous. Here she looks on at a classic-car show at the Hurlingham Club in West London in June 1998 with Yasmin Le Bon (left) and Lili Dent Brocklehurst.*

Firmly on the ground once more, Sophie picked up the threads of her career in promotional work and found herself a place to live. A well-connected and sporty neighbour from Kent, Ulli von Herwarth, had a spare room in her modest flat in Vereker Road, West Kensington, and Sophie took it. The rent of £350 a month was covered when she got a £12,000-a-year job working with Jill Phillips, the national promotions manager of the Cancer Relief Macmillan Fund based in Chelsea. Her organizational abilities as well as her experience with Capital Radio were put to good use in her role of researching and co-ordinating promotions to keep the charity in the public eye. Today Sophie still works for the fund as an active committee member, explaining, 'The Macmillan nurses do the most incredible work and I shall always have a special affection for them.'

When that contract came to an end she cast around for other work in the same field, sending her curriculum vitae to numerous public-relations companies. Her details landed on the desk of Brian MacLaurin, boss of MacLaurin Communications and Media (MCM), a dynamic media-management firm based in Hammersmith, not far from her home in W14. She was invited to an interview and MacLaurin, who once worked for Scottish TV, was immediately impressed. 'She had a lovely sparkle in her eyes. She was fun, gregarious, very easy to get along with, and had a solid track record,' he recalls. Sophie got the

job with MCM, and was quickly promoted to account manager. As a team player she fitted in well, working on the Noel Edmonds Garden Party Show, and the Lords Taverners and Thomas the Tank Engine accounts. There was no doubt that she enjoyed the somewhat ersatz glamour of mixing with TV stars and other celebrities at various publicity launches; however, it is an inaccurate, if well worn, popular myth that she handled Mr Blobby's PR. In fact, Sophie's most significant account was the Baby Lifeline charity, an organization founded by Judy Ledger, a formidable woman who has tragically lost three premature babies. Sophie became involved and the charity has since raised over £2.5 million for hospital equipment and neo-natal research. Judy has nothing but praise for the young PR girl who handled the account: 'Sophie is very determined and is so genuine in her interest in the charity.'

As if all this were not satisfying enough, even greater excitement lay ahead. Sophie had been with MCM for just a few months when Buckingham Palace called to ask MacLaurin to discuss promotional work for a charity project involving Prince Edward and his interest in real tennis. Fatefully, the wily Scot, MacLaurin, decided to bring Sophie along to the photo call at Queen's Club in West London.

Fortune smiled on Sophie as she poured herself into a white silk leotard and casually leant on Prince Edward's shoulder for a photo call. It seemed to

Behind the scenes at a charity real-tennis tournament in February 1994 – a nicely unguarded shot of Sophie and the Prince.

ABOVE LEFT: *Dressed in 1940s style, Sophie accompanies the Earl of Snowdon on their way to a formal engagement in 1997 to mark the golden wedding anniversary of the Queen and the Duke of Edinburgh.*

ABOVE CENTRE: *Sophie and Prince Edward arriving for an official engagement in December 1995 – quick to learn the niceties of royal protocol, she keeps the regulation two paces behind the Prince.*

ABOVE RIGHT: *Prince Edward's at times almost obsessive desire to keep the media at bay is not wholly unjustified. Here he and Sophie arrive for the wedding of Anastasia Cooke – whose name was once romantically linked to Edward's by the press – to James Baker in December 1994 beneath the baleful eye of the cameras. Sophie, for once, seems to have determined that 'Ladies first' will apply on this occasion.*

the whole world that they had known each other for years, and it remained the most intimate photograph of the couple until their engagement. Yet the love match would never have made it to the Centre Court had it not been for a hard-headed TV executive, a small-screen celebrity and a sassy publicity girl.

As has been mentioned earlier, PR assistant Sophie was drafted in at the last minute for a launch, on 13 September 1993, for Prince Edward's Real Tennis Summer Challenge charity, which was linked to the Duke of Edinburgh's Award Scheme (the Challenge itself being an endurance test for the participating players, who had to play on court for as long as possible). It had been planned that the original publicity photo would have been of the Prince with the tennis star Sue Barker, but when she had to withdraw the shoot was to have been cancelled. Prince Edward was at first uncertain when MacLaurin suggested that Sophie could stand in for Sue, but he instantly changed his mind when he saw her. The photo call went ahead, and the rest, as they say, is history. MacLaurin recalls, 'I've been many things in my time but I have never played Cupid before. However, there was no mistaking the chemistry that was between them right from the word go.'

During the day, Sophie had confidently demonstrated her abilities off court with her sharp ideas about how to promote the event and get the best press coverage. As a result she and Prince Edward kept in close professional contact, and she and MacLaurin were invited to meetings at the Prince's office at Buckingham Palace to discuss arrangements for the real-tennis charity. In the end the appeal successfully raised a handsome £29,000, and the ever hesitant prince suggested to Sophie that they might have a game of tennis 'some time'.

It was not until early October, however, that Edward started to make the running, on an occasion when he was guest of honour at a lecture in London to commemorate twenty years of commercial radio. Sophie was there too, and during the course of the evening Edward asked her for that game of real tennis. Even though Sophie later compared her performance on the court with that of a demented bluebottle, their match proved such a success that he invited her to his apartments at Buckingham Palace for supper. At some point Sophie served an ace by suggesting that she should take lessons in real tennis, with the result that one of the first presents he gave her was her own real-tennis racket.

Supper at the Palace was her first introduction to the physical hurdles of meeting royalty privately, as Edward briefed her on which entrance to use and his valet arranged with the police to allow her through the palace gates. Her verdict on his three-bedroomed apartment was that it was 'smart but not overbearingly regal'. As they chatted after supper she asked him quite simply, 'What do I call you?' The Prince laughed and replied, 'Edward, of course.'

This was, however, just the beginning of Sophie's crash course in royal etiquette. In November of that year Edward invited her to spend the weekend at his private apartments in the Queen's Tower at Windsor Castle. She was under the confident impression that she would not have to suffer the ordeal of meeting his formidable parents, having been told that they would be away. It was just a ruse. Once there, Edward told her that the schedule had been changed, and that after riding in the morning they were to have lunch with the Queen and the Duke of Edinburgh. In a spin of nervous trepidation Sophie sought advice from the Prince's valet, Brian. He told her when to curtsy, how to address

Sophie with Prince Edward in March 1996, attending the 5,000th performance of the Lloyd Webber hit musical Starlight Express. *By then, two and a half years after her first meeting with the Prince, the press were given to speculating heavily about an engagement.*

The Queen Mother, clearly delighted to see her grandson's girlfriend, greets Sophie at Scrabster Harbour, near Thurso in the far north-east of Scotland. The royal party then left for the nearby Castle of Mey, the Queen Mother's private residence on the coast of Caithness, which she bought in 1952 and renovated and restored.

everybody and what to call Prince Edward when talking about him in the third person. Edward had already rehearsed royal table manners with her, and told her how to cope with the butler service and the bewildering array of cutlery.

In due course luncheon was served. For Sophie, the dreaded moment had arrived. As she walked into the small dining room she was confronted by most of the royal family en masse – the Queen, Prince Philip, Princess Anne and her husband, Commander Tim Lawrence – who had all just returned from the Remembrance Day service at the Cenotaph. Yet despite her nerves, Sophie did not completely succumb to 'red-carpet fever', and her handshake and curtsy to the Queen were faultless. Most of the occasion passed in a blur, however, so that the most vivid memory she has is of the Queen rushing to the window to look at Concorde as it flew past. The following weekend Edward took her back to Windsor Castle, where she met the Queen Mother while attending a service at St George's Chapel. Sophie found that she was slightly more confident this time, although she was keenly aware of her extraordinary double life: two days earlier she had been sardined in the Tube on her way to work, and now she was in another world, staying in a castle with a prince and meeting his royal relations.

From now on the relationship moved up a gear. They spent many weekends of their courtship at Windsor Castle, and Sophie's natural give-it-a-go nature, and her willingness to join in quaint parlour games with the correct degree of gusto, struck the right note with the royal family. Back in town in her other life, the Prince took to calling her at her office two or three times a day. He used the false name Gus when he did so, no doubt after T. S. Eliot's Theatre Cat, but everyone knew who was calling.

Although Sophie felt totally at ease with the new man in her life, the social situation she was plunged into took some getting used to. Every time they

went out, Steve the detective came too, and if they drove anywhere she was always consigned to the back seat of the car, with Edward driving and Steve beside him in front. Yet while the romance was heightened by the necessary cloak of secrecy, Sophie felt increasingly ill at ease as they continued the elaborate public charade of a professional relationship. At the Lord Taverners Masked Ball, for instance, they both had to keep their distance throughout the evening. 'I really wish he wasn't royal, it just gets in the way,' she frequently lamented.

In fact, the couple's — and especially Prince Edward's — desire for secrecy was put to the test by Sophie's own family. When her brother David asked her about one of her weekends, she vaguely replied that she had been staying with

ABOVE: *Sophie arriving at Ascot.*

ABOVE RIGHT: *Still keeping just behind Edward's right shoulder — Sophie with the Prince at the wedding of Lord Snowdon's daughter, Lady Sarah Armstrong-Jones, to Daniel Chatto in July 1994.With under two months between them in age, Lady Sarah, one of his first cousins, was a close childhood friend of the Prince.*

some friends near Windsor. 'I hope you said hello to the Queen for me,' he joked. She realized then that she was going to have to say something to her family, and so, after consulting Edward, she decided to tell her parents the identity of her new paramour. (Her father, ever the joker, enquired, 'What is this young man's background? What do his parents do?') However, Sophie did ask her parents to counter any journalists' probing questions by replying that the relationship was purely professional. The Prince also briefed his senior staff at Buckingham Palace to that effect, although he was aware that both the Duchess of York and the Princess of Wales had a habit of leaking snippets to the press; there was, however, little he would have been able to do about that.

While Edward made careful plans to keep the media at bay, on one occasion that winter the couple and their close circle had great fun at the press's expense. Invitations to a shooting weekend at Wood Farm on the 20,000-acre Sandringham Estate included the instruction to bring warm clothes and 'some form of anti-photographer device such as a large floppy hat, headscarf or flamboyant wig'. The weekend was a huge success, not least because the party kept up a game of 'Hide the Sophie'. They made sure that when they were out tramping through the fields in view of the paparazzi the girls wore their wigs and floppy hats, while Sophie would swap walking partners; 'Anyone watch-

ing would have been totally confused,' recalls one of the guests. As it happened, none of the pictures of this strange crew appeared in the weekend papers because the Princess of Wales captured the headlines with her 'time and space' speech, in which she announced her withdrawal from public life.

Among the shooting party at Sandringham on the Saturday night, it had at one point seemed that Edward was about to make an even more dramatic announcement. After dinner he tapped the side of his glass for silence. Steve the detective had caught the speculation bug and put his head round the kitchen door and said, 'Hush, Prince Edward is about to announce his engagement!' For several seconds the guests held their breath in anticipation. Edward coughed and said, 'Not quite yet.' The party collapsed intó roars of laughter as the Prince thanked everyone for being such good company. But although the royal detective's timing was completely off the mark, by now the couple had declared their love for each other, and had discussed their future together. Edward was concerned about how Sophie would cope with the impact of media attention once their relationship was out in the open. Furthermore, his greatest ambition at this time was to build his television production company and lay some firm professional foundations before committing himself to married life.

When the story of Prince Edward and his new girlfriend finally broke just before Christmas of 1993, Sophie was staying at Windsor Castle. The Sunday

ABOVE LEFT: *A previously unpublished portrait of Sophie that has admirably captured her naturalness and ease before the camera.*

ABOVE: *At a City luncheon in aid of the Ireland Fund of Great Britain.*

RIGHT: *Sophie stayed on board* Britannia *for a time during the royal family's traditional annual cruise through the Western Isles in 1995. Here, Prince Edward's girlfriend has been snapped by a sharp-eyed photographer as, from the yacht, she watches the Queen arriving at Oban in the Western Highlands.*

BELOW: *Staying on* Britannia *during Cowes Week in July 1994, Sophie, always game for an adventure, tried water-skiing and windsurfing for the first time. She came to grief on both occasions: here, having fallen off water-skis in front of boatloads of photographers, she is helped into a launch — a photo opportunity she would probably rather had never taken place.*

papers are normally laid out by the Queen's place at the breakfast table, with the *News of the World* on top. When she read the headlines, Her Majesty commiserated with Sophie, regretting that this sort of coverage was one of the problems of being associated with her family. Prince Philip and Prince Charles also sent warm messages of support. For her part, Sophie made a statement at the time to royal biographer Andrew Morton: 'Prince Edward and I are good friends and we work together. He is a private person and so am I. I have nothing more to add.' Whatever she said, however, and whatever the royal family's support, the fact that the story was out marked a new stage in the relationship. Sophie would now have to suffer being hunted by paparazzi and press scavengers. She revealed later that she was very worried that she would be distanced from the Prince for the foreseeable future because of his great aversion to the press.

Sophie's official debut in front of a pack of the world's photographers as she went back to work that Monday morning was handled with consummate

style by her boss, Brian MacLaurin. The three television crews and fifty or so photographers failed to recognize her as she had restyled her hair since the real-tennis launch and they missed her as she swept into her office. They shot their target later in the day. While MacLaurin was looking after Sophie's press relations, Edward was drafting his open letter to editors pleading for the sort of privacy that had not been given to either of his brothers' relationships. He sent a detailed memo to Sophie and her parents warning them not to use hands-free phones, not to put rubbish out overnight, and never to drop their guard, because that is when the newshounds will pounce. Sophie had naturally become more reserved and cautious in public as the romance had blossomed, but she was secretly relieved that the news was now out in the open. The secrecy, the small subterfuges and little white lies, were all beginning to take their toll.

If this was a stern enough test, Sophie's worst ordeal since meeting Edward was also at the hands of the press, and came about when, in June 1994, the *Mirror* got things comprehensively wrong, running a story about the couple with the headline 'It's Off'. She heard the latest on the demise of her relationship on the car radio on her way to meet Brain MacLaurin for a charity event for disabled children; 'She was,' he recalls, 'genuinely very upset.' She showed her mettle, however, when she said a few words to the assembled hordes of journalists, during which she was unable to resist remarking, 'One of the reasons I like working with you guys is that I don't know what I'm going to read next.' It was an Oscar-winning performance, and one for which she summoned every ounce of stage technique learnt in her school days.

FACING PAGE, ABOVE AND BELOW: *Sophie at the launch of Callaghans, an Irish bar and restaurant established in the Cumberland Hotel near London's Marble Arch. The bar is dedicated to racing, which explains the memorabilia and the presence of Gerry Robinson (far left) with, next to him, Peter O'Sullevan and (on Sophie's left) Richard Dunwoody and Patrick Dempsey.*

RIGHT: *Prince Edward's fiancée takes her seat for the Five Nations Championship rugby match between Wales and Ireland at Wembley early in 1999, after the engagement had been officially announced.*

BELOW: *The front cover of* Hello! *magazine, 4 November 1995. At the time, the magazine's involvement in a gala evening in aid of Baby Lifeline, one of Sophie's favourite charities, threatened both her job with MCM and her cordial relations with the royal family. Her sensitivity — and good sense — in dealing with the conflict of interest left everyone satisfied, while her commitment helped to raise a considerable sum for the charity.*

The *Mirror* made up for its gaffe by printing a series of stories and pictures of Edward and Sophie together, but the fiasco prompted the couple in their decision to emerge from hiding and be seen about as a 'royal couple'. They let it be known that Sophie's parents would be joining the Queen at Balmoral in August that year, and they themselves were seen at the wedding of Lady Sarah Armstrong-Jones to Daniel Chatto that summer. Sophie's first official engagement as royal partner was at the Royal Tournament in Earls Court. These three events marked a breakthrough in her progress as the girl at Prince Edward's side. However, when she and Edward reached this 'understanding' about being seen together in public, she can have had no idea that her freelance status would last another four years before she could join the 'Royal Firm' on a permanent basis.

The next photo opportunity proved to be a very tasty morsel for the hungry press. A few days after the rather formal visit to the Royal Tournament, Sophie was invited to spend the weekend on the Royal Yacht *Britannia*. She had no hesitation in having a go at windsurfing and water-skiing. Her enthusiasm did not quite match her skills, and it became a case of 'welcome overboard' as she came to grief on both occasions, taking an undignified dunking in the Solent in front of boatloads of photographers, and at one time being rescued by one of the press launches. It seems likely that she will think twice about public displays of risky water sports in future.

Sophie has endeared herself to the most demanding members of the royal family. She has benefited from the full weight of the Queen's approval, even being allowed to travel to church in the same car as Her Majesty, unlike any other royal fiancées. She is a team player who will not be an embarrassment. She is extremely conscious of her public profile and she regularly sees the Queen to seek her advice, a quality that has earned her much praise inside the royal family. One such occasion pre-empted her losing her job with MCM, and shows the delicate balance between making the right move and slipping on a banana skin. In October 1995 Sophie had been compromised by a feature in *Hello!* magazine concerning her professional and personal interest in Baby Lifeline, one of her favourite charities. *Hello!* promised to produce £25,000 worth of sponsorship for the charity, the quid pro quo being that the promotion was to include a gala dinner with Sophie and Prince Edward. She had therefore been manipulated into a very awkward corner. If she declined the charity would lose out. If she appeared at the dinner it might have looked as if she was taking advantage of her royal connection in order to generate publicity, something she and Edward had in fact spent years avoiding. The Queen was very pleased to have been consulted, but was unperturbed. Sophie solved the problem by persuading *Hello!* to shift the focus of the event away from her and on to the charity. In the event the gala evening, held at the Earl of Bradford's stately home, Weston Park in Shropshire, was a triumph, and Sophie had the satisfaction of knowing that she had manoeuvred a tricky situation into a sparkling success; what was more, Edward was indeed there on her big night to give her his full support.

So it was with considerable regret that, not long after this, Sophie handed in her notice at MCM; she simply could not risk being forced into this position again, and she therefore took a lower-profile job promoting her favourite good causes. In 1997, however, she teamed up with business partner Murray Harkin to launch their public-relations company, R-JH, employing eight people at its Mayfair offices. It was a very astute move and the company has proved extremely successful, with an upmarket list of clients that includes the Lanesborough Hotel, Mayfair designers Thomas Goode, and French blue-chip consortium Comité Colbert, among a dozen others. The list reflects a lot of hard work, although Sophie's elevated social position certainly acts as a draw, and her efforts and ideas have placed her in the same income bracket as her husband. Nor has she any intention of taking the easy option and giving up her job after the wedding. Murray Harkin does not think marriage will make any difference to her desire to carry on; as he says, 'She's hard-working, always networking, always out getting business.'

Undoubtedly she has lived through some lonely moments, unsure whether she would play a mere walk-on part in Prince Edward's life story. At times their circle have been convinced that there would be no wedding at all. In 1998 eagle-eyed friends were reported to have discerned a certain frostiness between them, and on one occasion Sophie's absence from a house party at Sandringham was reported in the press as a sure sign that they were no longer 'an item'. She resented the loss of face and the implications that she had been jilted, but their relationship continued to meander along, and Edward was frequently reminded of his duty to Sophie, and of the fact that his casual behaviour might ruin her prospects if he did not make his mind up soon. The plain-speaking Duke of Edinburgh twice lectured his son on this very point. In January 1997 Sophie and Edward did in fact throw an engagement party to which they invited only close friends, but they then failed to make any announcement! At every turn any thoughts the couple had about announcing their intentions were scuppered by further instalments in the Greek tragedy unfolding in the rest of his family. Sophie sat tight and fully supported Edward's desire not to prompt headlines about his own betrothal just to mask the media emphasis on the grief of three divorces and, so suddenly in August 1997, the tragic death of the Princess of Wales.

ABOVE: *Murray Harkin, Sophie's business partner and co-founder of R-JH, the public-relations company they set up together in 1997.*

FACING PAGE ABOVE: *On the day of the formal announcement of their engagement, 6 January 1999, Sophie obligingly rests her hand on Prince Edward's arm so as to let photographers get a good shot of the ring. It is an exquisite triple-diamond band commissioned by the couple from the royal jewellers, Asprey & Garrard. The centrepiece is a 2.05-carat stone set between two heart-shaped gems. In 1997 Edward gave Sophie a gold signet ring engraved with her family's lion crest, as a symbol of his love.*

FACING PAGE BELOW: *Five years and four months after they first met, Sophie's smile says it all as she and Edward face the media on the day of their engagement.*

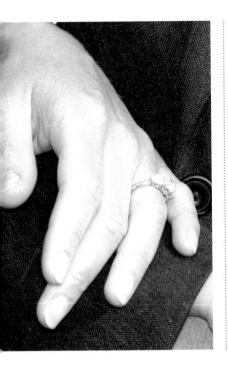

The tabloids remain intrigued by Sophie's passing resemblance to the late Princess. They share similar blonde hairstyles and a certain upturned glance; in practice, however, the two royal daughters-in-law could not have been more different. Sophie has a maturity gained by travelling the world, earning her own living and paying her own rent. She does not feel driven to replace Diana as the 'People's Princess', or to become 'Queen of Hearts'. She is unlikely to devote a great deal of her time to New-Age remedies, aromatherapy or colonic irrigation, and she is more likely to play a jolly game of tennis rather than punish herself at the gym. In short, she is no prima donna, and there should be no gaffes, no emotional outbursts and no overdraft problems. Her instincts, both professional and personal, are for survival and self-preservation.

Sophie is no longer waiting in the wings. She has made a subtle shift from normality to royalty, from supporting role to leading lady. It may only be a short taxi ride from W14 to SW1, but socially it is a million miles, and she has been put to the test every inch of the way. As she emerged into the summer sunshine with her husband, Her Royal Highness Princess Edward knew that her long journey to the altar had been worth every step.

❧ *Royal Weddings* ❧

Although the royal wedding as a public event is a relatively recent addition to the repertoire of kingly spectacles, these ceremonies have become central not only to the royal family in its attempts to win or keep public approbation, but also to the media, both domestic and international, which is only too well aware that royalty can and does attract millions of readers or viewers or listeners. A part of the reason for this is that such marriages are not only unions of two people, but also affairs of state in which pomp, pageantry and press attention have become integral parts.

Until quite recently the emphasis used to be on the public aspects of the partnership, but in the last two decades or so the House of Windsor has endured many changes. Furthermore, public interest has increasingly focused on the painful separation rather than the joining of two people in matrimony. In the case of Prince Edward's wedding, however, the occasion has been staged with more discretion, and to this end he has taken an unprecedentedly close personal hand in how the event has been covered and promoted. It may be, therefore, that after more than a century, the royal-wedding spectacular has come full circle.

For hundreds of years the unions of British monarchs and of their children were, if ceremonial, relatively private affairs, conducted in royal chapels, and much later in the day than is the custom – or, indeed, than is legal – nowadays. It was for the marriage of Queen Victoria and Prince Albert that the time of day for the wedding was changed from evening to afternoon. Since then the hour has been further shifted to the morning, and during the course of the twentieth century royal weddings have very often been held in Westminster Abbey (a famous exception being that of Prince Charles and Lady Diana Spencer, who were married in St Paul's Cathedral). The tradition of displaying the newly wed couple on the balcony of Buckingham Palace was another innovation of Queen Victoria's, when, on the occasion of her daughter Princess Victoria's wedding, she felt a twinge of pity for the crowds thwarted of getting a glimpse of the bride.

Before Queen Victoria brought royal weddings – literally – into the daylight, they had tended to be private and rather informal occasions, despite the diplomatic manoeuvrings and political exigencies that lay behind them, and which all too often brought together the most ill-suited distant royal cousins. There have been occasions, however, when there were good reasons for discretion. Edward IV, who reigned from 1461–70 and then from 1471 until his death in 1483, kept his marriage to Elizabeth Woodville in 1464 a secret because he did not dare tell his own council that he had married a widow and, worse, a commoner. It was to be five months before he admitted to the marriage. His fears were confirmed, for the union was deeply resented. After the King's death in 1483, his marriage was declared invalid, although Henry VII later restored Elizabeth as Queen Dowager.

Thereafter royal marriages were contracted between royal houses, and it was not until Queen Victoria's fourth daughter – and sixth of her nine

FACING PAGE: *King Charles II, a portrait from the studio of J. M. Wright. The King's deeply tactless, if honest, remark at the wedding of his niece, Princess Mary, to Prince William of Orange in 1677 was, at best, stonily received. Charles himself had married the refined Princess Catherine of Braganza in 1662, though his later treatment of her was cruel in the extreme, in marked contrast to the rewards he heaped upon his mistresses and his bastards.*

children – Princess Louise, married a commoner, the Marquess of Lorne (later ninth Duke of Argyll), in 1871, that customs began to change. From that time Britain's royalty have not looked exclusively to other royal families for the provision of their spouses. The only previous official royal marriage with a commoner was that of Charles II's brother, James, Duke of York, later to reign briefly as James VII and II until deposed by his son-in-law and nephew, William of Orange, in the 'Glorious Revolution' of 1688. In 1659 James 'entered into a private marriage contract' with the Earl of Clarendon's daughter, Lady Anne Hyde, though there was a political element to the match, for the Earl was chief adviser to Charles II. Again this union was kept under wraps for as long as possible, and once it was discovered the jealousy of the nobility was inflamed, especially as Anne became mother to two future queens, Mary II and Queen Anne. On his wife's death in 1671 James married another commoner, and a foreign one to boot, Mary of Modena. After the deaths of six children in infancy, she bore him a son, James Francis Edward Stewart, later to be known as the 'Old Pretender'.

As for James's daughter Mary, she married her first cousin, the Dutch Prince William of Orange, in 1677 in a ceremony conducted at nine o'clock at night in her own bedchamber at St James's Palace. The King, Charles II, attended, and, as Alastair Burnet relates, 'when he heard William promising to endow her with all his worldly goods, he told his niece loudly, "Put it all in your pocket, for 'tis clear gain." The remark was not appreciated. So, marrying her sister Anne to Prince George of Denmark at the Chapel Royal, St James's in 1683, [Charles] insisted there should be neither ceremony nor ostentation.'

To a casual observer, it must sometimes seem almost axiomatic that the first duty of a Prince of Wales is to dissipate the popular affection and respect gained by his parent, the Sovereign. (The behaviour when each was Prince of Wales of both Edward VII and his grandson, Edward VIII, immediately comes to mind.) This was certainly true of George III's irresponsible eldest son, who from 1810 ruled as Prince Regent in place of his mentally incapacitated father, and on the latter's death in 1820 succeeded him as George IV. In 1785 Prince George secretly married a twice widowed Roman Catholic commoner, Mrs Fitzherbert, although their union was declared invalid under the Royal Marriages Act of 1772, and the Prince later denied that he had married at all. Notwithstanding this rebuttal, Mrs Fitzherbert remained his mistress. In 1795, however, she talked him into marrying the florid and buxom Princess Caroline of Brunswick as part of a campaign to persuade the House of Commons to pay his enormous debts; an added bonus being that the rather less than fragrant Caroline would be no threat to the charming merry widow. The Prince conceived an instant, deep and lasting hatred for Caroline on meeting her for the first time on the day of the wedding; horrified, he immediately sought twenty-four hours' solace with the brandy bottle. Since there were at least three people in the Prince's marriage, one of them was bound to suffer, and George treated his wife, now the Princess of Wales, most cruelly: she was made to live by herself away from Court; when he succeeded to the throne in 1820 she was not officially recognized as Queen; she was turned away from his coronation at the door of Westminster Abbey; and

Sir Joshua Reynolds's painting of the wedding of George III to Princess Sophia Charlotte of Mecklenburg-Strelitz in 1761, which was held on the evening the Princess arrived in England. In the last 337 years, Britain has seen the marriages of only three reigning monarchs — those of Charles II, George III and Queen Victoria.

references to 'the Queen' were removed from the Prayer Book. When she refused an offer of a substantial sum to renounce her royal title and go and live abroad, divorce proceedings were brought against her, requiring a Divorce Bill to be passed by Parliament. But although her conduct was not altogether untouched by scandal, her husband's cruel treatment ensured a wave of popular sympathy and support, and the bill was dropped. Her triumph was short lived, however, for she died, supposedly of a broken heart, in 1821, her death attended by a great outpouring of public grief.

Despite his hatred of her, Queen Caroline did bear George a child, a daughter, Princess Charlotte, born in 1796. When, in 1816, she in turn came to marry, she simply had dinner with her grandmother, George III's widow, Queen Charlotte, and her aunts, before driving swiftly to Carlton House for the ceremony. (In 1761, as Princess Charlotte of Mecklenburg-Strelitz, her grandmother had been hastily married at night to George III on the very day she arrived in London from abroad.) Perhaps it was as well that the ceremony was in private, for the royal bride laughed out loud when the impoverished Prince Leopold of Saxe-Coburg repeated, 'With all my worldly goods I thee endow.' Her mirth notwithstanding, the bright, lively and good-natured Princess Charlotte was happy in her marriage, and her untimely death just over a year later, after giving birth to a stillborn boy, provoked another national outburst of public mourning.

After the excesses of George IV – and of his at times equally dissolute brothers, one of whom succeeded him when he died in 1830 and reigned as William IV until his own death in 1837 – the dignity and reputation of the monarchy were in dire need of restoration. This was the great achievement of Victoria and Albert. It was Queen Victoria who, recognizing her own high standing in the eyes of her people, made the first small concession to public curiosity.

Princess Alexandrina Victoria of Kent was born at Kensington Palace on 24 May 1819, the only child of Prince Edward, Duke of Kent, the fourth son of George III, and Princess Victoria Mary Louisa of Saxe-Coburg-Saalfeld, widow of Prince Emich Charles of Leiningen. She was not yet eleven years old when she learned that she might succeed to the throne, since neither of

Queen Victoria's wedding to Prince Albert of Saxe-Coburg and Gotha in the Chapel Royal, St James's, in February 1840. The painting is clearly romanticized, for The Times *called the chapel 'not much larger than the principal apartment of a catacomb' – indeed, it barely seats a hundred people. The success of the occasion, which drew the crowds despite wet weather and a paucity of ceremonial, led gradually to an acceptance of the idea that royal weddings should be treated as great public spectacles.*

her uncles, George IV and his brother the Duke of Clarence, later William IV, had any surviving legitimate children. Famously, she is said to have replied: 'I will be good.' Seven years later, in June 1837, William IV died and his niece succeeded to the throne. She was a month past her eighteenth birthday, and would reign for another sixty-three years. By the time she died, aged eighty-one, in January 1901, she had become a familiar figure not only to her British subjects, but to millions of others throughout the vast Empire that had been expanded and consolidated during her reign. The image that endured was of a small, rather rotund old woman, stern-looking and given only rarely to smiling, and invariably dressed in black since the death in 1861 of her beloved husband, Prince Albert, to whom she was, in Gladstone's words, 'in deed and truth, a second self'. Throughout the nearly forty years of her widowhood, she strove always to maintain the ideals and standards of the German princeling she had married when they were both aged twenty, and their blissfully happy marriage remains one of history's great royal romances.

In fact, the early auguries for the match might not have been thought all that auspicious, since it was effectively an arranged marriage, as had long been the custom among royal houses. Albert's uncle, Prince Leopold, Duke of Saxe-Coburg, later King of the Belgians (and whose first wife had been Victoria's cousin, the hapless Princess Charlotte), was anxious that his nephew should marry Victoria – to whom Leopold was also uncle – not least because marriage to the heir presumptive to the throne of Britain would immeasurably enhance the power and prestige of the House of Saxe-Coburg. Their engagement was announced in November 1939, and in February the following year they were married at the Chapel Royal, St James's Palace – the last time this country has seen the wedding of a reigning monarch.

In the event, the day of the wedding was wet. In her journal for that day, Monday, 10 February 1840, Victoria managed to describe two of the features that would become central to the whole royal-wedding extravaganza – her dress, and the crowds who turned out to watch, although the use of closed carriages because of the wet weather meant that there was actually very little for anyone to see:

> I wore a white satin gown with a very deep flounce of Honiton lace. I wore my Turkish diamond necklace and earrings, and Albert's beautiful sapphire brooch. Mamma and the Duchess of Sutherland went in the carriage with me. I never saw such crowds of people as there were in the Park, and they cheered most enthusiastically . . . I returned alone [in a carriage] with Albert; the crowd was immense; they cheered us most warmly and heartily; and the Hall at Buckingham Palace was full of people; they cheered us again and again.

The Queen set a new trend in royal wedding ceremonies by having twelve bridesmaids to carry her train, which was eighteen feet long; she was also the first English bride to wear her veil off her face during the service.

If the marriage proved to be a triumphant success from the start, it took a good deal longer for Prince Albert to gain the acceptance, let alone the approval, of many of those around the Queen, and among other slights he was refused a seat in the House of Lords. However, the well-educated Albert, a man of wide-ranging interests and high moral ideals, became permanent adviser to the Queen, who both admired him and relied upon him, although his fine qualities were not generally appreciated until after his early death from typhoid fever in 1861, at the age of only forty-two. Before then, the Queen and the Prince set a new standard for the conduct of the monarchy that has ever since been honourably observed by reigning monarchs of the day, though not always by princes. (The exception, the uncrowned Edward VIII, reigned for so short a period that his behaviour can be judged more as that of a private person, if an extraordinarily privileged one, than of a king.) Only in recent years have Victorian values of royal life been challenged and, in some cases, questioned or completely abandoned.

Given the hole-in-corner, if not clandestine, nature of royal weddings before Queen Victoria's, something of the success of hers – which would have been, by twentieth-century standards, a very thin public spectacle indeed – seems to have struck a chord in the Queen, as it was to do to a much greater extent in her grandson, George V. More than that, the chance to see, in some way to be involved with, royalty struck an answering chord among her subjects. Even so, royal weddings continued to be relatively low-key affairs, despite the increasingly huge numbers of people who turned out to see such spectacle as there was. When the Princess Royal – the Queen's eldest child, Princess Victoria – married Prince Friedrich Wilhelm of Prussia (later, albeit very briefly, the Emperor Friedrich III of Germany) at the Chapel Royal in 1858, many commentators contrasted unfavourably the lack of pageantry with the vast numbers of people who had come to see what little they could. The processional route from Buckingham Palace to St James's and back was the shortest imaginable (the Mall, purposely designed for ceremonial, was not completed until 1914), the chapel so small as to verge on the poky (it barely seats a hundred), and the crowds so dense that anyone not at the front had difficulty in seeing anything at all. Something of the public's disappointment seems to have communicated itself to the Queen, however, for on the royal party's return to Buckingham Palace she brought the bride and groom out on to the balcony to acknowledge the cheers of the crowd, thereby setting a precedent that has continued ever since, and incidentally creating what Alastair Burnet calls 'the essential royal wedding picture'. The marriage itself proved a happy one, although the first-born child of it, Prince Friedrich Wilhelm Viktor Albert, later the Kaiser Wilhelm II of Germany, would help to bring about the destruction of much of Europe, as well as being the chief cause of the conversion of the British royal family's surname from Saxe-Coburg Gotha to Windsor.

Prince Albert's death three years later drove his widow into a habit of mourning that she was never to abandon; from that time she wore only black, and even wrote her letters upon black-edged writing paper. Finding public events painful, she moved out to Windsor, although she remained as active as ever in affairs of state. Even so, her withdrawal produced a critical reaction – albeit a suitably deferential one – in her subjects, for whom the monarch and her family were at once a focus for their loyalty and a source both of pride and of undying fascination. As a result, for some ten years a hitherto almost unthinkable notion, republicanism, was actively and openly discussed in Britain. With a reclusive and clearly heart-broken Queen, as well as a somewhat dissolute Prince of Wales (whom Victoria thought frivolous and indiscreet and was inclined to blame for the Prince Consort's death, and

The wedding of Edward, Prince of Wales, later Edward VII, to Princess Alexandra of Denmark at St George's Chapel, Windsor Castle, in March 1863. Queen Victoria, still in deep mourning for her husband, Prince Albert, who had died some fifteen months earlier, watched the ceremony from the gallery in the chapel. The Princess wore a shimmering, bouffant-skirted wedding dress of white silk and silver

tissue, trimmed (as her new mother-in-law's had been) with Honiton lace, in a patriotic (or more likely, diplomatic) pattern of roses, thistles and shamrocks. Her looped pearl and diamond necklace (now a favourite of Queen Elizabeth, the Queen Mother), earrings and a brooch were a present from Edward. Again like her mother-in-law, she wore a wreath of orange blossom.

whom she excluded from affairs of state for a considerable time), what was needed was a policy of promoting royal occasions as a counter to public dissatisfaction with royal behaviour.

Instead, the next great royal occasion, the wedding in March 1863 of the Prince of Wales, later Edward VII, to the beautiful Princess Alexandra, daughter of King Christian IX of Denmark, served only to underline the Queen's determination neither to bow to the public taste for royal spectacles, nor to make too much of the event itself. Her attitude was at best questionable: the marriage of the heir to the throne was, and is, an event of great and enduring significance, as the wedding of Prince Charles to Lady Diana Spencer in 1981 proved all too well. But having ensconced herself with her grief outside

London, Queen Victoria refused to accept that her choice of St George's Chapel, Windsor Castle, for her eldest son's wedding would not meet with general approbation. In spite of widespread criticism about the lack of pageantry at Princess Victoria's wedding, once again the public was disappointed; suggestions that Westminster Abbey or St Paul's Cathedral would be more appropriate for the heir fell on deaf ears, and thus it was that the ceremony was held in what *Punch* called an 'obscure Berkshire village, noted only for an old castle with bad drains'. There was no grand, glittering procession through the capital for the Prince, although the Danish royal party, traversing five miles of London in order to reach Paddington station, brought people out in their thousands. For the rest of it, the day saw just a few sparsely decorated carriages in a little place outside the great capital, and though onlookers filled the streets, few were lucky enough to see the Princess.

However many daughters-in-law she might accumulate, the Queen felt the loss of her daughters acutely when they married foreign princes and moved away. In an age when was much made of rank and position, ambitious royal families still arranged politically and socially advantageous marriages for their sons and daughters. Such was Victoria's sense of isolation from her family, however, that she changed the rules governing royal marriages. At a time when it was still frowned upon for royalty to marry outside the hallowed and exclusive Courts of Europe, she began actively to seek husbands for her younger daughters from among the non-royal sons of the aristocracy, and in 1871 she decided that the fourth of her five daughters, Princess Louise, might marry a non-royal, the Marquess of Lorne. Thus Queen Victoria opened up the field of selection for potential royal spouses that would be to the great advantage of the monarchy for many years to come.

Her grandson Prince Albert Victor, eldest son of Edward VII and Alexandra, died suddenly in 1892, placing Prince George Frederick in direct line of succession; Prince George also inherited his brother's fiancée, Princess Victoria Mary (May) of Teck, and they were married in July 1893 at the Chapel Royal, St James's Palace. Succeeding his father on his death in 1910, King George V won the respect and love of his subjects – if not his sons, to whom he was a stern, unbending and sometimes choleric father – but his reign was not an easy one. He set a fine example in the First World War (one of his personal sacrifices was to give up strong drink except cider until the war's end), although the years after the Armistice in 1918 were marred by much political upheaval and by civil disturbance at home and abroad. He recognized early in the war, however, that Great Britain and the Empire needed a royal family untainted by connection with the Kaiser, and that the German influence in the name of the royal house of Saxe-Coburg Gotha had to be removed. H. G. Wells's reference to 'an alien and uninspiring Court' cut him to the quick – 'I may be uninspiring but I'll be damned if I'm an alien,' he quickly responded. In 1917, therefore, George V decreed that the royal family would henceforth be known by the surname of Windsor. (Others with royal connections and German names did the same, including Prince Louis of Battenberg, whose wife was one of the old Queen's granddaughters, who changed his family's surname to Mountbatten at about the same time.) The King's decision was greeted with approval by public and press alike.

The Duke and Duchess of York, later King George VI and Queen Elizabeth (now the Queen Mother), photographed at Buckingham Palace after their wedding on 26 April 1923. This was the first time that a son of a British king had married a commoner (although this is to ignore George IV's voided marriage, as Prince of Wales, to Mrs Fitzherbert). The bride wore a waistless wedding dress of ivory silk crêpe, rather medieval-looking, with strips of silver lamé embroidered with seed pearls, and with two trains, one from the hips, one from the shoulders. Her wedding ring was the first to be made from a single nugget of Welsh gold from which those of both the present Queen and Princess Margaret, as well as Princess Anne and Diana, Princess of Wales, were also made.

Princess Patricia's Canadian Light Infantry earned its reputation during the First World War, and remains one of the most famous fighting regiments in the world. Yet the royal princess after whom it was named – and who embroidered its first colour herself – has slipped into obscurity. Her marriage, however, just a few months after the end of the war, was perhaps the first royal wedding recognizably to receive the full treatment of pomp and press attention. Princess Patricia, daughter of the Duke of Connaught, was another of Queen Victoria's granddaughters; moreover, after her aunt, Princess Louise, she was the next member of the royal family to marry a non-royal. The nation had been rent by the First World War, only recently ended. Here, King George V clearly believed, was something to celebrate, an opportunity to put on a show of pageantry to brighten up Lloyd George's somewhat dismal 'land fit for heroes to live in'. Princess Pat, a relatively minor member of the royal family, was much loved by the public, and the fact that she was marrying a commoner – Commander the Hon. Alexander Ramsay, RN, a younger son of the thirteenth Earl of Dalhousie – may have added to the event's appeal to the public, given the changing social attitudes of the time, accelerated by the war. The ceremony, held at Westminster Abbey in February 1919, was the first royal wedding to take place there for some six hundred and fifty years. Excited crowds lined the streets – including the finally completed Mall – or perched themselves on any vantage point that allowed them a view over the sea of spectators. The first royal wedding – interestingly, of a minor royal and to a commoner – to be conducted with what now came to be considered due pomp and circumstance was proved a success.

Three years later, in February 1922, came the marriage of George V's beloved only daughter, Princess (Victoria Alexandra Alice) Mary, to Viscount Lascelles (later sixth Earl of Harewood). In view of the popular enthusiasm that greeted the previous one, this royal wedding was, from day one, held up to the public eye. A VAD during the war, and subsequently a nurse at London's Great Ormond Street Hospital, Princess Mary meant more to the nation than if she had been just any remote royal figure, and, fired by the newspapers' regular reports on the coming wedding's details, the crowd's excitement had reached fever pitch by the actual day.

Once again a sumptuous affair, the procession to Westminster Abbey was filmed – now a royal wedding could reach beyond those who crowded into London to catch a glimpse of the spectacle, and would be preserved for future generations, a major step towards modern communications technology. Photographs appeared not only in British newspapers and magazines but also across the Atlantic. In Britain the wedding dress was previewed by the manufacturers along with the Princess's trousseau and the wedding cake, while in the United States interest was almost as intense; after the wedding, copies of the dress were instantly put on sale in New York stores. On the day the couple were greeted by crowds of wildly cheering subjects in a display almost hysterical with loyalty and patriotism. But if the wedding set a pattern for almost all those that have followed, it was just the beginning of the royal story that was going to run and run.

The sense of participation, of involvement, in royal affairs that these displays gave to the nation served to increase the popularity of the royal family, of a king who was coming to be seen as a 'people's king', an image encouraged by George V's queen, Mary, who, like her husband, was sensitive to the nation's mood. With George V came the democratizing of the monarchy: among much else, he created a great many new peerages to break the power of the Tory House of Lords (although it is said that when approached with the idea that he should raise a number of people to dukedoms, he refused with the remark, 'What – add to that bunch of sh–ts?'), and in 1924 he gave his support to the first Labour government under Ramsay MacDonald, for whom he felt a sincere friendship. Of George V John Buchan was to write: 'What struck me was his eager interest, his quick apprehension and his capacious memory . . . Soberly and unrhetorically it can be written of him that he loved humanity . . . He was immensely considerate to all those who served him.' As Governor-General of Canada in 1936, Buchan himself, by then Lord Tweedsmuir, was to play an important part in advising the British government that Canada would not tolerate a King married to a divorcée.

Princess Elizabeth and the newly created Duke of Edinburgh in the Throne Room at Buckingham Palace after their wedding at Westminster Abbey in November 1947. Cheated of the wedding of Edward VIII by his abdication, the public thronged to this, the first royal spectacle of any note since the coronation of George VI in 1937, and the first since the war's end. In a time of shortages and drab austerity, 'Worn, Shabby Britons Thrill to Cavalry, Bands, Coaches', noted the New York Times.

It was not long before George V had another wedding to stage, that of his second son, Bertie – Albert, Duke of York – who in January 1923 became engaged to Lady Elizabeth Bowes-Lyon, daughter of the fourteenth Earl of Strathmore. (They had met in 1920, and she had, as it happened, been one of Princess Mary's eight bridesmaids.)

Bertie and Lady Elizabeth (now Her Majesty Queen Elizabeth the Queen Mother) were married on 26 April 1923. Under a bright sun, the Glass Coach carried the bride and her father from their London home along streets bordered by the million-plus people hoping for an early view of the bride, to Westminster Abbey. Described by the newspapers as 'a modest little Scotch girl', in fact, the old-established aristocracy, to which the Strathmores belonged, was such that a friend remarked with perfect seriousness that

Elizabeth was marrying beneath her. She displayed, on this very first day in public, her ability to do the right thing, to touch the hearts of the people. Later, on the Palace balcony (the tradition begun by Queen Victoria) to show herself to the populace, she blew a kiss to the thousands of faces looking up at her, a gesture that won many hearts.

Whatever the success of the wedding, however, *The Times* was still moved to comment that, 'There is one wedding to which they look forward with deeper interest – the wedding which will give a wife to the heir to the throne, and, in the course of nature, a future queen to England and to the British peoples.' The heir apparent was Edward, Prince of Wales, commonly known as David, and his marriage was a matter of great concern to George V, although even then the King was probably beginning to have his doubts about there being any such happy outcome where his eldest son was concerned. Nor would he live to see it. Instead, the next of his four surviving sons (the youngest, John, died in 1919 at the age of thirteen during an epileptic attack) to be married was Prince George, Duke of Kent, whose wedding in 1934 to Princess Marina of Greece also took place in Westminster Abbey; among the bridesmaids was the elder of the Duke of York's two daughters, Princess Elizabeth. Then, in November 1935, came the marriage of Prince Henry, Duke of Gloucester, the King's third son, to Lady Alice Montagu-Douglas-Scott, which was to have been held in the Abbey as well. The sudden death of the bride's father, the Duke of Buccleuch, however, led them to tone down the occasion, and they were married instead in the private chapel at Buckingham Palace. The Duke of York's daughters, the Princesses Elizabeth and Margaret, aged nine and five respectively, were bridesmaids, in Empire-style dresses designed, like the bride's, by Norman Hartnell – with one adaptation urged by George V, who wanted them shortened so that he could see his granddaughters' 'pretty little knees'.

On the evening of the Gloucesters' wedding, the King wrote in his diary, 'Now all the children are married except David.' Not long afterwards he wrote to the Prime Minister, Stanley Baldwin: 'After I am dead, the boy will ruin himself in twelve months.' The words proved more prophetic than even the shrewd old King could have guessed: in January 1936 he died, aged seventy-one, and was succeeded by his son David as Edward VIII who, just under eleven months later, abdicated in favour of his brother, the Duke of York.

Blessed with the common touch, the eldest of George V's four sons, Edward, Prince of Wales, was a popular man of the people and a firm supporter of the working classes. He was quickly dubbed the world's most eligible bachelor and lived up to such a reputation by attracting adoring women wherever he went. Aged nearly forty-two when his father died, and still unmarried, he was widely regarded as charming, yet weak-willed and indecisive – although his one crucial decision would change the course of history. That year, 1936, turned out to be the year of the three kings. The Prince of Wales acceded to the throne in January, and the country was able to look forward to the spectacle of the first marriage of a reigning monarch since Queen Victoria. However, on 11 December 1936, after only 325 days on the throne, the newly proclaimed King announced the unthinkable in a radio broadcast heard by millions throughout the world. 'I have found it impossible to carry the heavy burden of my responsibility and to discharge my duties as

An open State Landau carries the Prince of Wales, with one of his two supporters, Prince Andrew (the other being Prince Edward), to his marriage to Lady Diana Spencer, July 1981. Unlike most weddings of senior royalty this century, the ceremony took place at St Paul's Cathedral, which allowed an extended procession that brought people to the streets in their hundreds of thousands. The event attracted a worldwide television and radio audience of some 1,000 million people, greater than for any previous royal wedding, and very likely for any that may follow.

King as I would wish to do,' he said, 'without the help and support of the woman I love.' That woman was a twice divorced American, Wallis Simpson.

Although this wildly romantic decision cost Edward his birthright and his country, he found no difficulty in squaring the circle. 'She promised to bring into my life something that wasn't there,' he explained in his 1951 autobiography. 'I was convinced that with her I'd be a more creative and useful person.' The couple met while she was still married to Ernest Simpson, and Edward was conducting an affair with the married Thelma Furness. In time Ernest retreated into the background and Wallis found herself in a new and fairy-tale world of cruises and castles; 'It was like being Wallis in Wonderland,' she once observed. During his short reign Edward set about removing the one obstacle to his happiness – the Simpson marriage.

What all this hinged upon, of course, is the fact that British monarchs, as Heads of the Church of England, are forbidden to marry those who have divorced. In his speech on the Abdication in December 1936, the Prime Minister, Stanley Baldwin, explained how he started receiving 'a vast volume of correspondence', mostly from Britain, British subjects abroad and Americans of British origin, but also from the Dominions, 'all expressing perturbation and uneasiness at what was then appearing in the American Press . . . I felt it was essential that someone should see His Majesty and warn him of the difficult situation that might arise later if occasion was given for the continuation of this kind of gossip and criticism, and the danger that might come if that gossip and criticism spread from the other side of the Atlantic to this country.'

The Prime Minister went in October to see the King at Sandringham, where, 'talking it over as a friend', he expressed his worries. 'I told his Majesty that I had two great anxieties: one, the effect of a continuance of the kind of discussion that at the time was proceeding in the American Press; the effect it would have in the Dominions and particularly in Canada, where it was widespread; and the effect it would have in this country.' His other worry was the damage inflicted to the integrity of the monarchy, of such importance at the time 'as it is not only the last link of Empire that is left but the guarantee in this country . . . against many evils that have affected and afflicted other countries . . . Once lost I doubt if anything could restore it.' A month later, Baldwin went to see the King again: 'I told him that I didn't think that a particular marriage would receive the approbation of the country.' 'I am going to marry Mrs Simpson and I am prepared to go,' the King replied. Edward's own account of his meeting with Baldwin in November 1936 underlined the dilemma: '"I intend to marry Mrs Simpson as soon as she is free to marry," I said. If I could marry her as King, well and good; I would be happy and in consequence a better king. But if, on the other hand, the Government opposed the marriage . . . then I was prepared to go.' A few days later, however, the King suggested that perhaps he could marry Simpson and Parliament could pass an Act 'enabling the lady to be the King's wife without the position of Queen.' 'I told him,' reported the Prime Minister, 'that my first reaction was that Parliament would never pass it.' Urged by the King to examine his proposal, Baldwin agreed to do so, but eventually concluded that there was no prospect of such legislation being accepted. Mrs Simpson herself, in a signed statement read to journalists at Cannes, said that she was 'willing if such action would solve the problem to withdraw forthwith from a situation that has been rendered both unhappy and untenable'. Edward, however, would have none of that: 'I have determined to renounce the throne to which I succeeded on the death of my father, and I am now communicating this my final and irrevocable decision . . . I would beg that it should be remembered that the burden which constantly rests upon the shoulders of a sovereign is so heavy that it can only be borne in circumstances different from those in which I now find myself.' So it came about that on 11 December 1936 Albert, Duke of York, reluctantly succeeded to the throne as George VI.

'The throne,' said Edward, 'means nothing without Wallis beside me.' It is hard to believe now that, before the Abdication, there was no public comment in Britain about the King's affair with his American inamorata. In strict deference to the monarchy the British press adhered to its self-imposed censorship regarding the private lives of the royal family, with the result that very little was known about the affair, although it was widely reported abroad. When the news broke, therefore, the public felt a profound sense of shock and, to a very considerable extent, of betrayal. Having abdicated, Edward was keen to marry as soon as Mrs Simpson's divorce came through in April or May 1937, but Wallis thought it would be more fitting to wait until after the coronation of the new King on 12 May. The wedding date was therefore set for 3 June.

The marriage of the Duke of Windsor, as he was to be known, to Wallis Warfield (some weeks earlier she had resumed her maiden name by deed poll) was conducted by a rogue vicar from the North of England, Dr Jardine, who was acting in defiance of his bishop, and took place in the music room at

At the start of the marriage service, Lady Diana Spencer processes up the aisle of St Paul's Cathedral on the arm of her father, Earl Spencer (who had only recently recovered from a brain haemorrhage). Princess Margaret's wedding to Antony Armstrong-Jones (later Lord Snowdon) in 1960 was the first royal wedding in which the actual service was televised. Whatever the hopes of the millions who watched Prince Charles wed the beautiful Lady Diana, however, the fairy tale turned sour, not only for the bride and groom, but also for the monarchy itself.

Candé, a borrowed château in the Loire Valley, which had been converted to a chapel for the day. The wedding was boycotted by the royal family, and the King would not authorize any of his courtiers or senior officials to be present; old friends, too – like Lord Louis Mountbatten, who was to have been best man – declined to attend. The new King had also announced that while his brother would be granted the title of honour 'His Royal Highness', his future wife would not be accorded either royal title or rank. The much reduced wedding ceremony was in marked contrast to the type of occasion that the Duke might have expected as a reigning monarch. The only British official present was the Consul at Tours; Herman Rogers gave Wallis away; and the Duke's congenial old companion, Major E. D. (Fruity) Metcalfe, late Indian Cavalry, acted as best man. There were just fourteen other guests. Despite achieving this nevertheless supremely happy moment, and remaining devoted to each other for the rest of their days, for the Windsors life ahead would be very different from all expectations. The Duke's family and the British Establishment had made it clear that they regarded him and his wife as outcasts, and Edward had been moved from centre stage to the wings, from head of state to gentleman of leisure. Such condemnation of his marriage, and, especially, his brother's attitude and actions, rankled with him for the rest of his life, and were a perpetual source of friction between him and the King, the brother to whom he had once been so very close.

The couple, now the Duke and Duchess of Windsor, left Britain for voluntary exile, settling in Paris in 1938, where they became known for their elegant dinner parties and arguably aimless life, although invitations to their soirées were avidly sought by snob, arriviste and tuft-hunter alike. 'You have no idea how hard it is to live out a great romance,' Wallis later told a friend.

Edward's resignation may have been his most valuable service to the kingdom that had been his birthright, taking into consideration his political activities and his Nazi associations after the Abdication. His drastic action forced George VI into an impossible situation, having to rebuff, time and time again, his older brother's hopes of rehabilitation both for himself and his wife. This litany of disappointment that had begun with the absence of any member of the royal family at Edward's wedding, and the refusal of HRH status for Wallis Simpson, continued with many rows over money, augmented by the dislike of the King's wife. Queen Elizabeth was never to forgive the two people whose actions had led to her husband becoming King, a role which, she believed, considerably shortened his life. The Duchess of Windsor was shunned by the royal family until Edward's death in 1972, when the Queen finally invited her to stay in Buckingham Palace.

More than sixty years on, Prince Edward himself has become the first member of the present royal family to comment publicly about the torment of the Abdication, in his television documentary about his great-uncle. He paints a broadly sympathetic picture of a misguided man who could not understand either the sense of betrayal felt by his former subjects or the ostracism from his own family. Trying to explain what drove the King to become a lonely exile, Prince Edward offers the only fair conclusion, 'We'll never know for sure whether it was supreme arrogance, utter disillusionment or blind passion.'

If the public had been cheated of the wedding of a reigning monarch – indeed, had been deprived of that monarch himself – it was to be royally rewarded some ten years later with a spectacle equalled only by George VI's coronation in May 1937. In February 1947, Prince Philip of Greece, only son of Prince Andrew of Greece and nephew of the deposed King Constantine I of the Hellenes, became a naturalized British subject. At the same time he changed his surname from Schleswig-Holstein-Sonderburg-Glücksburg to Mountbatten, in honour of another of his uncles, Lord Mountbatten of Burma (whose father, of course, had changed his family's surname from Battenberg). On 10 July the same year, the heir presumptive to the throne of Britain, Princess Elizabeth, announced her engagement to Lieutenant Philip Mountbatten, an officer of the Royal Navy who had served with distinction during the war. Her marriage to Philip, newly created Duke of Edinburgh (he was not made a prince of the British creation until 1957), took place in Westminster Abbey on 20 November – the first great state occasion since the

The Prince and Princess of Wales in an open State Landau on their way to Westminster Abbey for the wedding of Prince Andrew to Sarah Ferguson, July 1986. Their own wedding five years earlier had marked the beginning of the public's fascination with and adulation of the Princess, something that reached its apogee after her tragic death in August 1997.

war, and something to brighten up the bleak years of shortages and dashed hopes that followed victory. Under the orders of the King, who was all too aware of the nation's need for some splendour, the full panoply of royal spectacle was put on show for the first time since war was declared. The King's purpose was well served: not just the country, but the world was seized by a sense of the occasion – a young and good-looking couple; the charming heir to a monarch who had performed his duties so admirably during the war; above all, hopes in Britain of an end to the drab austerity that seemed to be all that victory had brought. Here, too, was something in which the media, with its rapidly burgeoning technology, could be fully involved – press, radio, film and televison (though cameras were not permitted in the Abbey) ensured that the wedding reached a worldwide audience of unprecedented size. At times, perhaps, the media were too intrusive: walking behind the bride, the first of Elizabeth's eight bridesmaids, Princess Margaret, just managed to catch one of her sister's two pages when he tripped over some broadcasting equipment. The event strengthened the affection and respect in which the King, Queen and royal family were held, something that reached far beyond the borders of the kingdom. Among the many wedding presents to arrive was Mahatma Gandhi's – a loincloth made from cloth he had woven himself upon his famous hand loom. The bride's grandmother, Queen Mary, was horrified.

Princess Margaret enjoyed the same upbringing as her conscientious sister the Queen, but without the responsibilities associated with the duty of succeeding to the throne herself. Although she has adhered to a strict set of royal rules, while for many years maintaining a maverick jet-set lifestyle, her private life has always been somewhat bohemian. She is the first modern royal to have been pursued by the press hungry for intrusive stories of her sometimes unhappy and unfulfilled relationships, and the first to have her private life discussed throughout the land. She has followed her own instincts in more recent times, but in the strait-laced 1950s when everyone was expected to do their duty to God and the Queen, the Princess found herself unable to marry her suitor, Group Captain Peter Townsend. The fact that he was divorced posed insurmountable constitutional and ecclesiastical problems, such were the conventions of the day; moreover, the memory of the problems that had followed Edward VIII's decision to marry a divorcée was still very fresh in both the public and the official mind. Townsend, a distinguished fighter pilot during the war, was a former Equerry and Master of the Household to King George VI, but he was posted abroad and became a gentleman-in-exile once the story broke that the Princess was in love with him. For the first time the press, and even some of the most erudite commentators, broke the rules of deference and dared to criticize the Princess's decision not to marry Townsend, in which she was supported by her sister, the Queen. She subsequently married the glamorous society photographer Antony Armstrong-Jones in a blaze of publicity and press interest. The glittering ceremony, held in Westminster Abbey on 6 May 1960, was the first ever royal wedding in which the actual service was also televised. Noël Coward, watching on television the departure of bride and groom on board *Britannia*, 'discovered, unashamedly and without surprise, that my eyes were full of tears.' Less sentimentally, though with greater prescience, one of the Princess's so-called well-wishers commented of the wedding, 'Marry in May and rue the day'; the couple were divorced in 1978.

In the same year Prince Michael of Kent married a divorced Roman Catholic, Baroness Marie-Christine von Reibnitz, in a civil ceremony at the Town Hall in Vienna. The stigma of divorce meant that he had to obtain special permission from the Queen, and renounce his right of succession to the throne – he was sixteenth in line.

Although never far from the gossip columns, Princess Margaret has since enjoyed the freedom to conduct her own characteristically unconventional private life while the media spotlight has increasingly been aimed at younger members of the royal family. The glare of the limelight has never been so bright as it was for the wedding of the heir to the throne, Charles, Prince of Wales, to Lady Diana Spencer on 29 July 1981. At the time, it seemed that the most eligible bachelor in the world had found his true love. Beguilingly shy and very beautiful, she appeared to be the perfect candidate for the role, adding some much needed glamour to the increasingly dour Windsor dynasty. It was to have been the wedding of the century, but the fairy tale turned sour, not only for the bride and groom, but also for the monarchy and, ultimately, the whole country.

While the family Diana was about to join may have been dauntingly formidable, the publicity she received was overwhelming. The worldwide television and radio audience for her wedding was estimated to be a record 1,000 million. Despite the best of British pomp and pageantry, and the endless rehearsals that are necessary to bring such events off, the nervous couple

*The Queen's second son, Prince Andrew —
created Duke of York by his mother just an hour
and a half before the service — married Sarah
Ferguson at Westminster Abbey on 23 July
1986. This photograph was taken after the
ceremony in the Throne Room at Buckingham
Palace, the photographer, Albert Watson, later
admitting that he had been much taken by the
Duchess's natural beauty. Sadly, their marriage,
like those of Prince Andrew's sister and elder
brother, also ended in divorce.*

muddled their words, as had both Princess Charlotte and Queen Victoria.
Diana confused Charles's name, and he promised to share with her 'all her
goods', instead of all his worldly goods. Perhaps these were ill omens; certainly the Archbishop of Canterbury unconsciously misled everyone when he
said the marriage was 'the stuff of fairy tales'. Before the wedding Diana said,
'I thought I was the luckiest girl in the world when I looked at Charles
through my veil. At the age of nineteen you always think you are prepared for
everything.' However, the naive young Princess was anything but prepared for
her new life. She recalled, 'No one sat me down and said, "This is what is
expected of you." But although I was daunted by the prospect at the time, I
felt I had the support of my husband to be.' While their lavish wedding
brought scenes of joy and celebration to a nation suffering from an economic
recession and recovering from unprecedented inner-city violence, it soon
became clear to the new Princess of Wales that a third person would be featuring in her marriage. Even on the honeymoon, photographs of Camilla
Parker Bowles would slip out of the Prince's diary, and when Charles arrived
for dinner with the Egyptian premier, Anwar Sadat, he was wearing cufflinks
decorated with two interwoven Cs. 'I could not see why Charles needed these

constant reminders of Camilla,' Diana told friends later. Nor was Camilla the only problem in the marriage, for not the least of the young bride's troubles was the twelve-year age gap. Even at thirty-two, Prince Charles seemed almost middle-aged, while he and his wife had wildly different characters and interests.

It was, however, apparent almost as soon as Diana appeared on the royal stage that she had an electrifying effect on the crowds, and the cameras loved her. She was a blank canvas on which the public could paint any image; she could be cover girl, media toy, sportswoman, angel of compassion, abused wife, single mother, queen of hearts, anti-landmine campaigner – almost everyone could identify with her. Her popularity grew until it literally had no bounds. So when the self-styled 'Prisoner of Wales' let her story be told in print in 1992 and subsequently agreed, after her divorce, to be interviewed on the BBC's *Panorama* in November 1995, the foundations of the monarchy shifted for ever. People would never again tolerate the requirements of the aristocratic marriage in which the well-bred husband was permitted to maintain his own interests along with his mistress (discreetly, of course), while the good wife kept up appearances and produced the heirs. In the no-nonsense nineties, hypocrisy and double standards in the lives of public figures would no longer be tolerated.

Since the beginning of Queen Elizabeth's reign in 1952, a time of discretion and deference, society has changed and the individuals within the royal family with it. The monarchy is an ancient institution that naturally resists change, but no one could have predicted the sad events that led the Queen to refer to 1992 as her *annus horribilis*. The divorce of Princess Anne and Mark Phillips, the separations of the Duke and Duchess of York and the Prince and Princess of Wales, along with the fire at Windsor Castle and mounting criticism of the Queen's exemption from paying income tax, all added up to a miserable year. The Queen's blessing of Princess Anne's second marriage to Commander Timothy Laurence, RN, in 1993 showed a fresh attitude towards divorce, but it undermined the official stand that had been taken against Princess Margaret's choice of husband in the 1950s. Yet to the public, and probably, if for more cynical reasons, to the media, the event that will be seen as the nadir of the decade is the tragic death of the Princess of Wales in August 1997.

It would have seemed remarkable to many people at the beginning of the century that royal weddings would be elevated to such a spectacle, second only to a coronation. However, today the rules governing royal marriages and the behaviour of princes and princesses have changed. Society itself has been undergoing a profound shift embracing a variety of cultures and creeds, with many new ideas about family values, especially divorce. It no longer respects appearances in the way it did only a generation ago. When the Queen allowed the television cameras to film her family in 1969 for the BBC's documentary, that family gave up much of its mystique. The bulk of the British public want the royal family to continue in their conventional role as symbols of national identity, but that identity has changed rapidly since the end of the Second World War, and especially during the latter part of Queen Elizabeth's reign. People no longer expect them to be perfect emblems, simply conscientious public figures; equally, people no longer regard them – except perhaps the Queen and the Queen Mother – with the same unquestioning loyalty, or

St George's Chapel, Windsor Castle, the scene of Prince Edward's marriage to Sophie Rhys-Jones on 19 June 1999. The chapel is a place of worship for the Sovereign and the royal family, and is also the Chapel of the Order of the Garter. Construction of the building was begun in 1475, under the reign of Edward IV, whose marriage to Elizabeth Woodville was conducted in such secrecy that it was only five months after the ceremony that he dared to tell his council.

accord to them the superiority that was once held to be their due. Perhaps more than that, however, the failures – and at times very public failures – of the marriages of the Queen's three older children, as well as that of her sister, have helped to add an at times cynical, if not hostile, edge to the public perception of royalty. It may no longer be possible for the splendour and solemnity of a royal wedding to unite the people in their affection for, and loyalty to, the royal family.

The new generation of royals are tailoring their standards to reflect less extravagant ideals, something that may, perhaps, enable them to lead relatively normal private lives. Other young married royals – Prince Edward's cousins, Lord Linley and Lady Sarah Chatto, for instance – and their spouses are by and large left alone by the press. In a cadet branch of the family the Hon. James Lascelles, great-grandson of King George V, has married a Nigerian, Joy Lemoine, who has been welcomed as the first black member of the royal family. It will remain to be seen how the media treat Edward and Sophie. After the decade of divorces, upheaval and much public debate about the very existence of the monarchy, perhaps they have wisely chosen to hold a personal and genuinely meaningful wedding in the family chapel at Windsor.

✑ The Wedding ✑

FACING PAGE: *What the world had hoped — and waited — for: a beautiful bride in a stunning wedding dress. Sophie smiles for the crowd as she arrives at St George's Chapel, Windsor Castle, maintaining the bride's traditional prerogative by being five minutes late.*

BELOW: *A royal bridegroom does not have a best man, but one or more 'supporters'. Their Royal Highnesses the Prince of Wales and the Duke of York escort their brother, newly created Earl of Wessex, through the precincts of Windsor Castle to St George's Chapel before the service — a pleasantly informal saunter that vastly pleased the waiting crowd.*

SATURDAY, 19 JUNE 1999, the day of the wedding, belonged to the bride, and true to her own style, Sophie dared to be different. At shortly after five o'clock in the afternoon, she became part of an ancient monarchy, playing the central role in a personal ceremony that set a new royal standard. For while such weddings have become the perfect medium for promoting the image of the royal family to the public, Sophie and Edward succeeded in staging the personal, intimate event that they had wanted. Yet this was also a national occasion — with a difference. The last royal wedding of the century showed a worldwide audience that the British monarchy is moving into a new era, paring down a number of carefully chosen traditional customs or transforming them with some very modern ideas. There were no echoes of the grand matrimonial occasions of the eighties, for the tone and style of what proved to be an uniquely satisfying spectacle was a discreet mix of ancient and modern. In the end, perhaps the most striking feature of this truly unconventional royal wedding was the way in which the couple followed the established form, yet added a new slant at every turn. And in that they were applauded by public and media alike.

It is a custom of the British monarchy for the Sovereign to award his or her sons a title either upon their coming of age, or upon their marriage. As a sign of affection for her youngest son, the Queen bestowed upon Prince Edward the title of Earl of Wessex, an ancient name last held at the beginning of the

millennium by King Harold II, who was killed by an arrow at the Battle of Hastings in 1066, the defeat that led to the Norman occupation of Britain. Edward will also inherit his father's title of Duke of Edinburgh upon Prince Philip's death. Thus, on the day she married, Miss Sophie Rhys-Jones became Her Royal Highness The Princess Edward, Countess of Wessex, at the moment she took her vows. She will be known privately as Sophie Wessex, and it was also announced that, in line with the royal policy for lower-ranking members of the family, any children of the match will not bear the style 'HRH'.

ABOVE: *For those invited into the castle precincts, as for the media, the spectators lining the route and the millions of televison viewers, this was their first glimpse of one of the central features of a royal wedding – the dress. The design chosen by Sophie and created by Samantha Shaw proved a triumphant success.*

Sophie conducted herself with consummate skill during the weeks leading up to her wedding day. With great composure and dignity she attended the marriage of Samantha Shaw, the designer of her own wedding dress, at the height of the storm of public disgust at the cruel publication in the *Sun* of *that* blurred old photograph. In dealing with the furore she once more demonstrated both her strength of character and her professional abilities, and emerged with her reputation greatly enhanced. She is trusted and admired by her husband's family, and is said to be the daughter-in-law Prince Philip has longed for. She is a very welcome new member of the royal family, and one who has shown that she will not be bowed by relentless press intrusion, not least because she is eminently qualified to play the media game – and win.

The now customary pre-wedding interview, filmed at their marital home at Bagshot Park, was a perfectly crafted piece of television. The couple spoke openly and with great eloquence to Sue Barker – most fittingly, since it was indirectly through the tennis star that they first met – about their courtship, their work, which is a priority for them both, and their public and private plans. Sophie is the first royal wife to work full-time at her own career, and she will continue in her role as Chairman of R-JH Public Relations. Yet she

FACING PAGE: *The Bishop of Norwich precedes Sophie and her father up the steps to the chapel's West Door, as pages and bridesmaids support the train and veil.*

ABOVE LEFT: *Camilla Hadden waves to onlookers while one of Sophie's two pages, Felix Sowerbutts, smiles as they approach the steps leading up to the West Door of St George's.*

ABOVE RIGHT: *Prince Edward is escorted into the chapel by Prince Charles who, showing something of his youngest brother's individuality, elected to wear grey morning dress.*

RIGHT: *Before the service, the bridesmaids were at times in danger of stealing the show — Olivia Taylor smiles enchantingly for the cameras.*

showed her commitment to the union by admitting that in her wedding vows she would promise to love, honour *and* obey her husband. This surprised some modernists, although it should not have done, for Sophie stated unequivocally that she trusts Edward to take decisions that will be for the good of them both. The couple's performance during the interview was confident and relaxed, and occasionally punctuated by joyous laughter. This was no awkward or over-boisterous prince and his bride-to-be discussing the meaning of love, but two clear-eyed people whose love has been tested and tempered by reality.

If their affection for each other spoke for itself, so too did their determination to do things in their own way. The choice of St George's Chapel at Windsor, scene of Prince Edward's confirmation in 1978, was a break with tradition, as was the choice of Right Reverend Peter Nott, Bishop of Norwich, to lead the ceremony in preference to the Archbishop of Canterbury; the Dean of Windsor, the Right Reverend David Conner, led the prayers. The Bishop, a friend of the royal family and a regular preacher at Sandringham, has known Edward for fourteen years and Sophie for five.

Windsor in Waiting

The press predicted little public interest in the wedding. But on the day, well-wishers arrived early to secure the best view, and enjoyed the June sunshine while waiting to catch a glimpse of the royal couple.

The day of the wedding was planned with military precision, but there was no guard of honour and only a minimal military presence, since Prince Edward no longer has any links with the armed forces; indeed, the Prince is the first royal groom in recent times not to have married in military uniform. The invitations had stipulated morning dress for men and evening dress – without hats – for the women guests. If this unusual dress code posed an interesting fashion challenge, it was an elegant choice for a wedding that took

The precincts of Windsor Castle on 19 June, before the wedding got under way: a balloon commemorates the event as crowds await the arrival of guests and bride around the statue of Queen Victoria outside the castle; hanging baskets are attached to posts outside St George's Chapel; members of the public arrive with chairs and picnics as they settle down to wait for the royal procession; the invitations, posted in the week beginning 3 May, also specified morning dress for men and evening dress for women; the programme of music and events in the last hour and a quarter before Sophie's arrival at St George's.

E R

The Lord Chamberlain
is commanded by
The Queen and The Duke of Edinburgh
to invite

to the Marriage of their son
Edward
with
Sophie

...hter of Mr and Mrs Christopher Rhys-Jones
at St. George's Chapel, Windsor Castle
on Saturday, 19th June 1999
at 5 o'clock
and afterwards at Windsor Castle

THE QUEEN'S FREE CHAPEL OF ST GEORGE, WINDSOR CASTLE

The Marriage of
His Royal Highness The Prince Edward
with Miss Sophie Rhys-Jones

PROGRAMME OF MUSIC AND EVENTS BEFORE THE SERVICE

¶*From 3.45 p.m., music is played by Telhard Scott Esq., Organ Scholar to the College of St George:*

Toccata & Fugue in F (BWV 540)	Johann Sebastian Bach (1685-1750)
Scherzetto (from Sonata in C minor)	Percy Whitlock (1903-46)
Villanella	John Ireland (1879-1962)
Fantasia & Fugue in G major	Sir Hubert Parry (1848-1918)

¶*From 4.25p.m., music is played by Roger Judd Esq., Assistant Organist to the College of St George:*

Fantasia & Toccata in D minor (op.57)	Sir Charles Villiers Stanford (1852-1924)
A Fancy	Sir William Harris (1883-1973)
A Song of Sunshine	Alfred Hollins (1865-1942)

¶*From 4.30 p.m. Royal guests begin to arrive at the West Door of the Chapel.*

¶*At 4.40 p.m. Her Majesty Queen Elizabeth The Queen Mother arrives by car at the Galilee Porch.*

¶*At 4.43 p.m. for the entrance of the Bridegroom, together with His Royal Highness The Prince of Wales and His Royal Highness The Duke of York:*

Allegro marziale	Frank Bridge (1879-1941)

¶*At 4.46 p.m. Mrs Christopher Rhys-Jones, the Mother of the Bride, arrives by car at the West Door.*

¶*At 4.50 p.m. for the Procession from the West Door of Her Majesty The Queen and His Royal Highness The Duke of Edinburgh, preceded by the Choir, the Minor Canons and the Dean and Canons of Windsor:*

Flourish for an Occasion	Sir William Harris
Prelude on Rhosymedre ("Lovely")	Ralph Vaughan Williams (1872-1958)

¶*At the arrival of the Bride, The Royal Band of Her Majesty's Royal Marines will play:*

Fanfare for Sophie	David Cole (b.1948)

¶*For the Bride's Procession to the Altar Screen:*

Marche Héroïque	Sir Herbert Brewer (1865-1928)

place in the late afternoon, and it meant that guests need not change their outfits before the evening dance began. On the day, Edward and his brothers, clad in morning dress, strolled informally through the precincts of Windsor Castle on their way to St George's Chapel, waving to the crowds. In another happy touch, as the guests arrived the sight of ladies in exquisite long dresses with shawls, boleros and chiffon scarves to cover their shoulders was both stylish and unusual.

Sophie's wedding dress was created by society designer Samantha Shaw, an individual choice that neatly avoided comparisons with previous royal brides. In keeping with tradition the dress was kept a closely guarded secret, only the smallest number of people having sight of it before the day. It did not

FAR LEFT: *Samantha Shaw, the designer of Sophie's wedding dress, adjusts Isabella Norman's dress prior to her marriage to Timothy Knatchbull in July 1998.*

LEFT: *Sophie attended Samantha Shaw's own wedding just days after the* Sun *published that photo, silencing all her critics by her courage and dignity.*

BELOW: *Three days before his marriage, Prince Edward was in Edinburgh to commemorate the twenty-first season of the National Youth Orchestra.*

FACING PAGE ABOVE: *Ruthie Henshall, a former girlfriend of Prince Edward's, arrives for the ceremony; Paul Burrell, formerly butler to Diana, Princess of Wales chats to a member of the crowd before the wedding.*

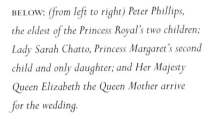

BELOW: *(from left to right) Peter Phillips, the eldest of the Princess Royal's two children; Lady Sarah Chatto, Princess Margaret's second child and only daughter; and Her Majesty Queen Elizabeth the Queen Mother arrive for the wedding.*

disappoint – the crowds applauded with admiration on first glimpse of the simple ivory dress as Sophie and her helpers arranged the organza and silk train before entering the chapel. The design was a sleek, panelled long dress-coat richly embroidered with 325,000 sparkling cut-glass and pearl beads. The veil, itself sewn with beads, trailed back and down to a length even greater than that of the train, and was held in place by a diamond tiara lent by the Queen from her private collection, while round her neck Sophie wore a

black and white pearl necklace and cross designed by Prince Edward, his wedding gift to his bride. The chosen florist, Sue Barnes of Lavender Green in Windsor, worked closely and discreetly with the couple and Samantha Shaw to create a bouquet which, she said, she wanted to match the stylish nature and romantic thoughts of the bride and groom. A new variety of tall lily named after Sophie was the main feature of her bouquet. With their characteristic attention to detail, the couple discussed every aspect of the occasion with Samantha and Sue, including the overall 'look' of St George's Chapel, right down to camera angles for the worldwide broadcast.

There were 550 guests in the chapel, and in keeping with a desire to make this a private occasion invitations went only to family, friends and colleagues from the worlds of business, theatre, media and sport. There were no politicians and only a small number of foreign royalty. The couple broke the rules again by choosing four non-royal children as bridesmaids and page boys. Entirely as was expected, however, Prince Edward chose both his brothers, the Prince of Wales and the Duke of York, as his supporters, a 'supporter' being the royal equivalent of best man.

Before the wedding, Sophie and her family had stayed at Royal Lodge in Windsor Great Park as guests of the Queen Mother. At the appointed time on the day of the wedding, Sophie and her father travelled from there to St George's Chapel in a 1977 Rolls-Royce Phantom from the Queen's fleet which had been decorated with a white ribbon, a first for this royal vehicle and a delightful common touch. The bride did, however, uphold one ancient custom by arriving at the chapel five minutes late. On the arm of her father, Christopher, she gave a shy smile from behind her veil as she ascended the twenty steps to the West Door to a fanfare especially written for her and performed by bandsmen of the Royal Marines – a nice touch, in view of the Prince's formerly rather unhappy association with that corps. The

Royal Arrivals

ABOVE LEFT: *The Queen Mother remains a striking and dauntless figure, even in her ninety-ninth year and less than twelve months after a major operation.*

ABOVE RIGHT: *The Duchess of Gloucester (right) walks up the steep incline in the castle precincts with her daughters Lady Rose Windsor (centre) and Lady Davina Windsor. Following them are Prince and Princess Michael of Kent.*

ABOVE: *Lord Snowdon, the former husband of Prince Edward's aunt, Princess Margaret, arrives outside the chapel. He and the Queen's sister were divorced in 1978.*

ABOVE: *Lady Gabriella Windsor, the eighteen-year-old younger child and only daughter of Prince and Princess Michael of Kent, known to her family and friends as 'Ella'.*

ABOVE: *Lady Helen Taylor, second child and only daughter of the Duke and Duchess of Kent. Born only a few weeks after Prince Edward, she was, and remains, one of his closest friends.*

BELOW: *One of the most enduringly popular members of the royal family, the Duchess of Kent, arrives for the service.*

BELOW: *The Hon. Sir Angus Ogilvy, husband of the Queen's cousin Princess Alexandra, who is the Duke of Kent's younger sister.*

BELOW: *Princess Anne's husband, Timothy Laurence, leaves one of the minibuses that were used to bring guests to the chapel.*

congregation in St George's sits in pews that face the aisle, thus allowing a perfect view of the bride as she walked up the aisle to her groom, waiting at the high altar. As she reached his side, Edward smiled warmly at her – and winked.

There were 8,000 ticket-holding, flag-waving members of the public, many from the local area in accordance with the couple's wishes, in the grounds of Windsor Castle, and many thousands more in the town itself. The hour-long service was relayed throughout the grounds on huge video screens and hymn sheets were given to all the ticket holders. The crowds cheered enthusiastically when Sophie first spoke – a joyous sound audible inside the chapel – and when the couple exchanged their vows and their Welsh gold wedding rings, at which the Edward and Sophie broke into broad smiles.

After the ceremony the couple stood for a moment on the chapel steps with their bridesmaids and pages but, with typical reserve, then dashed all expectations by resisting a public kiss, which had been such a feature of both his brothers' wedding photo calls. Then, only minutes later, they were driven from the chapel in an open Ascot landau provided by the Royal Mews, with postillions and outriders in semi-state livery; a second landau brought the bridesmaids, pages and Edward's two supporters. In the heat of a fine but slightly cloudy afternoon, this small procession wound its way through the streets of Windsor, passing through St George's Gate, down Castle Street and finally down the Long Walk to the castle itself, and so to the reception in the State Apartments. In yet another departure from royal precedents, this was followed by a buffet-style dinner – and, later, by dancing – in the magnificently restored St George's Hall, the Queen's pride and joy, and perhaps the symbol of the family's rebirth after the *annus horribilis* of 1992.

Above all things, this wedding has demonstrated the great goodwill and support for the couple among the public at large, and has underlined the fact that the newlyweds' mature and understated style is widely respected by a

THIS PAGE: *Followed by the Queen (above), the newlywed couple descend the steps at the end of the service. Sophie's bouquet was created around a new variety of tall lily which had been named after her.*

FACING PAGE ABOVE: *Pages and bridesmaids flank the royal couple as they pose briefly for photographs. Their outfits echo the robes and caps of holders of the Order of the Garter – of which St George's is the Chapel.*

FACING PAGE BELOW LEFT: *The Princess Royal and her eighteen-year-old daughter, Zara Phillips.*

FACING PAGE BELOW CENTRE: *Prince William stands between his younger brother, Prince Harry, and the Duchess of Kent.*

FACING PAGE BELOW RIGHT: *Prince Edward's new parents-in-law. Before the wedding they had stayed, with Sophie, as guests of the Queen Mother at her country house, Royal Lodge in Windsor Great Park.*

nation jaded by royal extravagance in both consumption and behaviour. Their Royal Highnesses the Earl and Countess of Wessex are ideal ambassadors for the British monarchy as it moves into a new era at the end of the twentieth century. They have shown that they have the personality and mutual

ABOVE: *The couple set out on the drive by landau through Windsor to the reception in the castle's State Apartments.*

LEFT: *A second landau followed, bearing Prince Edward's two supporters and Sophie's bridesmaids and pages. Camilla Hadden sits between Prince Charles and Prince Andrew . . .*

FACING PAGE ABOVE LEFT: *. . .While on the opposite seat Olivia Taylor looks out at the crowd, with Henry Warburton beside her.*

FACING PAGE ABOVE RIGHT: *Princess Beatrice, elder daughter of the Duke and Duchess of York, and Princes Harry and William, the two sons of the Prince and late Princess of Wales.*

FACING PAGE BELOW: *Landaus from the Royal Mews were each drawn by four greys, postillion ridden, with an escort of two Royal Mews outriders; postillions and outriders wore Ascot livery of top hats, red coats and white breeches, providing a splash of colour.*

OVERLEAF: *Their Royal Highnesses the Earl and Countess of Wessex leaving their wedding reception by car for the almost traditional 'secret destination'.*

determination to make this marriage a success. In themselves setting the tone for this stylish and surprising wedding, Prince and Princess Edward have struck a perfect balance between public and private, old and new. In this, perhaps, lies the hope, it may be even the salvation, of Britain's royal family.

❧ *Acknowledgements* ❧

With special thanks to Andrew Morton and Toby Buchan, and to Lorna Machray of PA Photos.

For readers who would like to learn more about the subject, I have found the following books useful:

RONALD ALLISON AND SARAH RIDDELL, *The Royal Encyclopedia*, Macmillan, 1991

THEO ARONSON, *Princess Margaret: A Biography*, Michael O'Mara Books, 1997

MICHAEL BLOCH, *The Duchess of Windsor*, Orion (paperback edn), 1997

JOHN BUCHAN, *Memory Hold-the-Door*, Hodder & Stoughton, 1940

ALASTAIR BURNET, *The ITN Book of the Royal Wedding*, Michael O'Mara Books
in association with Independent Television News Ltd, 1986

LADY COLIN CAMPBELL, *The Royal Marriages: Private Lives of the Queen and Her Children*, Smith Gryphon, 1993

PETER DONNELLY, *Diana: A Tribute to the People's Princess*, Bramley Books, 1997

GARTH GIBBS AND SEAN SMITH, *Sophie's Kiss: The True Love Story of Prince Edward and Sophie Rhys-Jones*, Blake, 1997

PAUL JAMES, *Prince Edward: A Life in the Spotlight*, Piatkus, 1992

ANDREW MORTON, *Diana, Her True Story – In Her Own Words*, Michael O'Mara Books, 1997

INGRID SEWARD, *Prince Edward: A Biography*, Century, 1995

EDWARD, DUKE OF WINDSOR (EDWARD VIII), *A King's Story: The Memoirs of HRH The Duke of Windsor*, Cassell, 1951

The author and publishers are grateful to the following sources for permission to reproduce photographs in this book:
Alpha Photographic Press Agency Ltd: 10 *above left*; Michael O'Mara Books Ltd: 13, 53, 64–5, 80 *left*; Crown Estate copyright: 51 *above*;
Rex Features Ltd: 58, 60, 61; *Hello!* Magazine, 83 *below left*; By courtesy of the National Portrait Gallery, London: 87;
The Royal Collection © Her Majesty Queen Elizabeth II: 89, 90–1, 92–3; *The Illustrated London News* Picture Library: 95, 99;
Camera Press, London: 97 (Baron), 101 (R. Slade), 105 (Albert Watson); Independent Television News Ltd: 103.

JACKET/COVER: *photographs, front and back* – PA Photos, London; *background, front and back* – the interior of St George's Chapel, Windsor
Castle, during the marriage of Queen Victoria's youngest son, Prince Leopold, Duke of Albany, to Princess Helen of Waldeck-Pyrmont,
May 1882. A detail from an engraving in the *Illustrated London News* of 6 May 1882 (The *Illustrated London News* Picture Library).

All other photographs were kindly supplied by PA Photos, London,
whose assistance is hereby gratefully acknowledged.